action of some kind. Many wonderful people have helped in this attempt by contributing their ideas, expertise, and time to create a working nonprofit organization called Thc Patients Party (see Chapter 17) whose mission is *to give patients a voice in the healing of healthcare and America.*

So, let us move forward together with humility, much humility.

Part I
Perspective

The political discourse about healthcare reform in America is absolutely frustrating. I am struck by how little discussion there is about *patients.* What I hear about almost all the time is *money.*

– *Anonymous*

Chapter 1
Walter's Words

Walter Cronkite once said that *America's healthcare system is neither healthy, caring, nor a system.* In the early autumn of my life, I found myself thinking just such thoughts.

I was in my sixties, very much enjoying and appreciating my work. At times over the years of my practice, I would experience moments of stress. However, the majority of my days were filled with poignancy and even laughter.

Most of all I was grateful to have had the kind of work that provided me so much opportunity to help people. However, those Cronkite-type thoughts kept surfacing.

Eventually I began to gain some clarity about our nonsystem of healthcare. The phrase *Assholistic Healthcare* popped into my head, and this became the umbrella under which I began to view the big picture. By 2010, I published *Assholistic Healthcare;* I wanted to share information about healthcare matters with all patients.

Publication of that book was a weigh station – a place to park for a while, but not a stopping point. By the time I reached my mid-seventies, I had written two more books about this; I thought of *Medicine's Moral Mess* and *The Answer to Medicine's Moral Mess* and *Dr. Medicare* as progress reports.

Rather than diminishing the allure of the path I was walking, the passion kept growing. I began thinking I wanted to contribute to constructive changes that would ultimately help all patients. I understood this would be a huge undertaking; I would laugh and ask myself, How the hell are you going to do this? I didn't have an easy answer.

Finally, I reluctantly concluded that the time and focus required to responsibly continue practicing was not compatible with passionately devoting my full effort to healthcare and compassion writ large. With regret, I decided to give up clinical practice.

Early on in the transition, I wrote a letter to my patients: "It has been a privilege and honor to have had the opportunity to share in so many lives through the years. In the future I will continue to work toward your best interests by spending time educating for change in our healthcare system."

The process took about eighteen months, with a December 31, 2018 retirement date. During this transition, I was able to devote more time to reading, exploring, writing, and developing a nonprofit organization called The Patients Party.

Writing this book has been a challenge because of the complexity and potential contentiousness of the topic. I've tried to write *Patients Before Profits* in a nonpartisan fashion; in our current hyperpartisan environment this is difficult. I've tried my best to keep things clear and civil. Civility is a central aspect of civilization. George Washington said it well: *Every action done in company ought to be with some sign of respect to those that are present.*

One of my psychiatry professors once said to me, "It is less important what you say to someone than what they hear." Winston Churchill nailed it: *These are my opinions on which I base my facts.* I agree that no human being can be completely objective and totally detached from personal perspective, whether consciously or subconsciously.

Many of us live in geographic areas that have some cultural and political bias. Furthermore, you might be surprised to learn that we are often biologically predisposed to tilt left or right. Skilled neuroradiologists can look at specific brain imaging of different people whom they know nothing about, have never met nor seen and never spoken to, yet with far better than random accuracy, predict who is Democrat and who is Republican.

I also know that our personal beliefs are not simply a reflection of our genes. We may each be genetically tilted, but biases or prejudices are not just hardwired or biologically wired. The environment each of us grows up in has a lot to do with how we turn out. We can change and sometimes do. But what we're taught, especially when young, our first five or six years when enrolled in Childhood University, modifies that biological tilt each of us has.

In this book, I share some of my core beliefs (perhaps prejudices) that I've developed over the years. I don't regard these "health subjectivities" as politically motivated; I regard them as pragmatically motivated. I might have facetiously said that these ideas are objective. That's ridiculous – not really possible. But I have tried to be reasoned and reasonable.

For example, it is easy to generalize and say you are for or against socialism or capitalism. I ask the impossible: Suspend your prejudice until you've read this book. I don't think this dichotomy is that simple. The Eskimos have about fifty words for snow. Semantically, economics probably should be more complex; we have too few words to carefully designate exactly what we mean when using the single words socialism or capitalism. I wish we had more nuance.

This said, there is one particular aspect of potential misunderstanding that I especially want to nip in the bud: *Patients Before Profits* is not intended to apply to all areas of American life. If I suggest that government is fairly efficient in healthcare, I am not suggesting that it is efficient in defense spending, education, or agriculture. If I suggest that government has a guiding role to play in healthcare, I am not suggesting that it should be engaged in manufacturing automobiles.

Healthcare should be personal, not political. I am not an advocate for big government; parts of government function well, parts do not. Far more than most of us realize, American society functions as a blend of socialism and capitalism. (I reflect on this in Chapters 7 and 12.)

I have spent more than fifty years of my life practicing medicine, and I am for putting patients before profits. I am for compassion.

Uwe Reinhardt, considered the dean of healthcare economics, dominated the field in America – and perhaps the world – well before his 2017 passing. *Priced Out: The Economic and Ethical Costs of American Health Care* was published posthumously and would have drawn me to Princeton to seek his counsel before the publication of *Patients Before Profits*. The reason

I so regret not knowing Professor Reinhardt will be clear as I share the first paragraph of the prologue to his book:

> "More and more Americans today are finding that health care has become increasingly expensive and, for many, unaffordable. Compared to national health systems in the rest of the developed world, American health care and the American health system are exceedingly complex and almost beyond human comprehension. As America faces such a crossroads where we must decide how we should proceed with our health care and health reform going forward, the need to understand both is great, especially now."

I present the ideas in *Patients Before Profits* not as a clairvoyant truth teller, but with at least a little comfort of having spent so many of my adult years in this arena. I am keenly aware that this book challenges some of the traditional thinking about American healthcare that has been drilled into most of us.

Fixing our healthcare dilemma will be challenging, but not because it's too complicated. Our lack of healthcare excellence reflects uneven access, misinformation, and our heated political partisanship rather than lack of capacity. In society and in our individual lives, difficulty and chaos can lead to positive change. Usually the optimist, I am hopeful that the painful coronavirus pandemic that we've endured will in some ways inform the development of improved American healthcare, one that Cronkite would have declared *is* healthy, *is* caring, and *is* a system.

There are people who have money and people who are rich.

– Coco Chanel

Chapter 2
Losing Hippocrates

During my years in medicine, I've been especially excited about advances in technology as well as advances in the understanding of genetics and the complex medical nature of human emotion. But I've been disheartened about the growing perception of medicine as a business more than a profession.

Some of my colleagues may seriously disagree with me. That's okay; I am not the arbiter of truth. As I've said, I always allow for my being wrong. However, acknowledging my fallibility and discomfort about touching some physicians with a grey brush, I would feel just as uncomfortable in writing this book and not being forthright about these issues. (Aspects of my discomfort arise in Chapter 8.)

Sometimes we physicians are put under pressure to produce income by organizations that employ us. Unlike the special interests, however, we physicians usually have no fiduciary responsibility to make more profit, but sometimes we don't act that way.

Some physicians justifiably complain of increasing costs of running a practice driven by insurance company paperwork hurricanes, often ridiculous and cumbersome, requiring more employees, and producing an unconscionable theft of physician/patient time.

Whatever the causes, over the past thirty or so years, insidiously, perhaps subconsciously, we seem to have been sliding down the profit-business rabbit hole. The willingness of many of us to regard medicine more as a business and less as a profession is our choice, and possibly our shame.

I am grateful to have had the opportunity to

practice medicine. Despite my frustration about the business direction of medical practice, the vast majority of my colleagues deserve serious respect. Most physicians work hard and shoulder heavy responsibility, often involving profound life and death issues that weigh heavy; and I do believe most physicians care.

Some hospitals, pharmaceutical companies, insurance companies, and other special interests don't seem to care if patients are suffering, as long as they have a way to protect their profits. Yet in fairness and in our market mindset, unlike physicians, many businesses do have a fiduciary responsibility to maximize profits for shareholders. We may want these businesses to care, and to be more socially responsible, but up to now, that has not really been their ballgame.

Often, despite best efforts, services are denied. Without extraordinary perseverance by the physician and staff, a certain percentage of seemingly valid claims are never paid by insurance. The result of this Machiavellian insurance strategy is not only the inflation of our cost of practicing medicine, but also the inflation of out-of-pocket costs for patients, and the inflation of insurance company profit by paying for fewer goods and services. This is malignant rationing. (See Chapter 7). It was about twelve years ago during the discussion that followed a medical dinner that I asked my colleagues, "Do you think we have gradually become less than ethical in our practice of medicine?"

First, there was dead silence. I waited. Finally, a lone voice asked, "What do you mean?"

"I mean, I find myself wanting to prescribe a particular medicine that I believe would be best for my patient, but I don't because it's not covered by their insurance. Or I believe a stay in the hospital would be in a patient's best interest, but I know insurance wouldn't cover it in today's climate, so I don't try. There are undoubtedly other examples, but overall I've begun to feel that sometimes I haven't stood up for patients, that I've allowed things to happen that I believe or know are not in the patients' best interest. I've wondered if we're honoring our Hippocratic Oath."

There was again quiet and then a few tepid comments like, "I guess I see what you mean, but I don't feel we're unethical."

Hippocrates was a Greek physician who lived about 2,500 years ago and is regarded as the father of modern medicine. The Hippocratic Oath is administered to most doctors when they receive their medical degree. I do not remember what version of the Oath I spoke when I became a doctor in June of 1968. Some medical schools use a version that was written in 1964 by Dr. Louis Lasagna, then academic dean of Tufts Medical School. I decided to review that version to remind myself what I promised.

As you read the Oath, take note that it does not contain the oft-cited phrase *primum non nocere* or "first, do no harm." That phrase is said to have originated from the teachings of a prominent French pathologist from the eighteenth century. What the Oath did contain that I had completely forgotten was a promise to *"pay attention to the patient's family and economic stability."*

Hippocratic Oath

> I swear to fulfill to the best of my ability and judgment this covenant: I will respect the hard-

won scientific gains of those physicians in whose steps I walk, and gladly share such knowledge as is mine with those who are to follow.

I will apply for the benefit of the sick, all measures [that] are required, avoiding those twin traps of overtreatment and therapeutic nihilism.

I will remember that there is art to medicine as well as science, and that warmth, sympathy, and understanding may outweigh the surgeon's knife or the chemist's drug.

I will not be ashamed to say, "I know not," nor will I fail to call in my colleagues when the skills of another are needed for a patient's recovery.

I will respect the privacy of my patients, for their problems are not disclosed to me that the world may know. Most especially I must tread with care in matters of life and death. If it is given me to save a life, all thanks. But it may also be within my power to take a life; this awesome responsibility must be faced with great humbleness and awareness of my own frailty.

Above all, I must not play at God.

I will remember that I do not treat a fever chart

or a cancerous growth, but a sick human being, whose illness may affect the person's family and economic stability. My responsibility includes these related problems, if I am to care for the sick.

I will prevent disease whenever I can, for prevention is preferable to cure.

I will remember that I remain a member of society, with special obligations to all my fellow human beings, those sound of mind and body as well as the infirm.

If I do not violate this Oath, may I enjoy life and art, respected while I live and remembered with affection thereafter. May I always act so as to preserve the finest traditions of my calling and may I long experience the joy of healing those who seek my help.

As I read this modern version, I felt sadly sure that during the years I have been studying and practicing, medicine's connection to the spirit of Hippocrates has faded. Whether consciously or not, some of us have come to define ourselves more as business people than medical professionals.

The Healing of America by T.R. Reid provides an in-depth review of healthcare in other industrialized nations. What touched and troubled me most was his observation that the way a country deals with healthcare reflects its moral values. According to Reid, the rest of the industrialized world does not understand us. There is undoubtedly a bit of schadenfreude as other nations take pleasure in how the exceptional United States has managed to build a healthcare system based upon the world's best medical science and technology, and yet construct from that largesse a bloated fiscal engine with so much wasteful spending and inefficiency.

Where is our soul where healthcare is concerned? You may be very uncomfortable and dislike considering that others think of America like this. But according to Reid, many do where healthcare is concerned.

I began to discuss my concerns about our healthcare system with medical colleagues. Because large numbers of uninsured and underinsured patients are financially unable to access care for routine problems, medical crises develop.

I spoke about this with one of my friends and mentors, Dr. Alan Halperin, who recently retired and is now professor emeritus of internal medicine at the University of Florida. Until very recently, for many years, one of Alan's responsibilities as professor was to serve as chairman of the Institutional Review Board. All medical universities have such a board in order to screen proposed medical research for scientific and ethical integrity.

Alan and I frequently talk healthcare. As he is always very thoughtful, I asked him to write about his university experience. In characteristically concise fashion, this is how he responded:

> "Some in the media and in politics have mistakenly portrayed the uninsured as illegal aliens or lazy freeloaders who choose not to have insurance. My experience does not support this prejudiced and stereotypic view. I'm not surprised that this distortion has occurred. Such people are often invisible to many of us whose lives are more fortunate. They are especially invisible to many physicians who do not treat them because as patients they cannot afford to pay.
>
> In my university practice, I often saw these

uninsured or underinsured patients. They are mostly hardworking people providing necessary basic work such as clerical, cleaning, and construction services. Some are self-employed and uninsured. Many work for small businesses that do not provide healthcare. When they develop an injury or illness, they often cannot continue working. Without access to care, they are unable to obtain the needed operations, medications, and physical therapy required to restore health. The downward spiral begins."

The extra cost of caring for a patient in crisis, or not in crisis but without access in healthcare except the emergency room, is one of many factors that send our medical costs through the roof. And there are significant human costs as well, such as protracted illness, premature death, disruption of families, interruption of employment, and homelessness.

The intent to be compassionate toward our fellow man is not a partisan issue. Compassion is not Republican or Democrat, Libertarian, conservative or liberal, rich or poor, Christian, Jewish, Muslim,

Hindu, Buddhist, Shinto, or any other religion. It is about being a loving, caring human being. By decreasing attention to our responsibility to protect patients' best interests, we sully our commitment to the fundamental meaning of being a physician. To varying degrees, we have allowed our plowshares of professional integrity to be forged into swords of profit.

In the weeks before my previous book *Dr. Medicare* became available to the public, and approximately three days after the Jacksonville beaches were notoriously opened to the public, I became a beach witch. I carried a broomstick and occasionally extended it (with a smile) to remind strollers on the beach to maintain appropriate social distance during this COVID-19 era. I was walking with two of my colleagues: Alan Halperin whose words you just read, and recently retired cardiologist Randy Wainwright. The day was beautiful, the beach was wide, flat and not overcrowded, the breeze was gentle, and we were all wearing masks.

During our stroll we had a chance encounter of the pandemic kind with Mark Mcintosh, a quadruple board-certified (internal medicine, pediatrics, emergency medicine, and palliative care) University of Florida medical colleague of Alan's who I also knew. The few times time I've seen Mark, I found his electric intellect stimulating. During the course of our relatively brief conversation that day, he said something that better translated my feelings than the words I had spoken twelve years ago when I raised the question of ethicality. "I know just what you're talking about. I'd put it slightly differently. Lately the pandemic has focused my thinking about the ragged disorganization of the American healthcare system. I find that our system draws us (physicians) into areas of medical practice that violates our moral compass." Alan, Randy, and I all agreed.

To hell with public vs. private, capitalistic vs. socialistic, Republican vs. Democrat vs. Libertarian vs. Independent, or single payer vs. multiple payer. What matters is whether you, your children, parents, brothers, sisters, and friends can wake up each morning knowing that excellent affordable healthcare is readily available without fear of financial distress or ruin. What matters is that our national economy is not ravaged by the impact of the profound financial inefficiency of our patient-hostile delivery system. If healthcare is to truly become exceptional in America, we must change our system from the ground up. Patients are more important than money. Emerson said it best: *Without a rich heart, wealth is an ugly beggar.*

The great enemy of truth is very often not the lie – deliberate, contrived and dishonest – but the myth – persistent, persuasive and unrealistic. Too often we hold fast to the clichés of our forbears. We subject all facts to a prefabricated set of interpretations. We enjoy the comfort of opinion without the discomfort of thought.

Let us not seek the Republican answer or the Democratic answer, but the right answer. Let us accept our own responsibility for the future.

–John F. Kennedy

Chapter 3
Patients Before Profits

When I first began this healthcare exploration, I did not start out with the intention of writing about healthcare reform or compassion; I wanted to write about the erosion of values in modern medicine.

Since my teens I've viewed life as a poem, with verses that are unique to each of us. I stumbled into this major new verse of my own poem about a dozen years ago, when I asked my medical colleagues: *Do you think we are practicing medicine ethically?*

Most current healthcare discussions lack any serious consideration of this issue, perhaps because of tacit acceptance by all sides that the political and business complexity of current medical practice necessitates some *ethical elasticity*. I should have realized from the beginning, however, that values and healthcare are, or should be, inextricably related.

Daniel Kahneman's insightful book *Thinking Fast and Slow* explains that our conscious thought processes are far from the whole picture of our brain function. A lot of power lies below the surface in our subconscious; as a psychiatrist this is familiar territory. In fact, I've often told my patients, "If life was simply logical, I'd be out of business."

As I think back to that evening when I asked about our ethical behavior, my subconscious thinking seemed to erupt from a deep geyser in the aquifer of my soul. It was unplanned.

At the time, I had been studying and practicing medicine for more than forty years and had written a couple of books related to the misunderstanding of psychiatry.

Suddenly something shifted. I began to look at

a bigger picture of healthcare and ask myself if our American system was really okay. I concluded that our system had serious shortcomings. I wondered if my patients felt this way, so I began to ask them.

There seemed to be a general perception that we had problems, but not much clarity as to what those problems were. As I began seeking answers and focused on the increasingly heated national healthcare debate about the Affordable Care Act, I became annoyed.

I heard such misinformation from so many politicians and pundits that I wondered if they or I had been living in some sort of alternative universe. I felt some were unintentionally providing bad information because they were ignorant, while others knew damn well that they were providing bad information in order to support their political agenda. Whatever the intent, misinformation causes harm. Partisanship flourishes. All the while, many Americans are being victimized, either healthwise, financially, or both.

Despite the United States not seeing fit to provide coverage for all citizens, we manage to spend more money per capita on healthcare than every one of our fellow nations who do provide healthcare insurance or access of one kind or another to everyone. There's a sad irony to this. By many measures, while our fellow nations spend much less, in *every* instance their overall healthcare performance is better. Over the years, when I discussed this, the one thing many people found hardest to swallow was the notion that our system was not the best (see Chapter 5).

For those of us who do have reasonable insurance and know how to navigate the system, excellent care is available. However, if you do not have government-supported healthcare (Medicare, Medicaid, the VA, Tricare, the U.S. Public Health Service) as do active duty military, federal workers, many state employees, either you or your private employer may pay an excessive amount of money to provide you access to private insurance that is often weak.

For about a third of our citizens, that huge group with no insurance or very poor-quality insurance, healthcare is not so great. It's the poor access and inconsistency of care in this large group that pulls our overall healthcare performance down.

The power brokers in healthcare have been the

special interests such as drug companies, insurance companies, and hospitals – all with lots of money. Not surprisingly, they buy a lot of influential media that provides messaging intended to promote more profit and fertilize the notion that American healthcare is the best in the world. They also influence Congress with expensive lobbying and campaign contributions.

Although most patients individually do not have the money for lobbying or major campaign contributions sufficient to influence our elected representatives, we patients control all the votes that the special interest money is ultimately intended to influence. Isn't that ironic?

I realized that despite the power of special interest money, once there is a groundswell of patients who decide they want to change healthcare, or anything else, the collective vote trumps special interest dollars. I will never again underestimate the importance and power of my vote.

Many factors contribute to our mediocrity, one of which most of you would never identify – the abject failure of the free market in healthcare. Market function is not always as ideal as some would suggest; but in healthcare the problem is particularly ugly. (See the whys and wherefores in Chapter 6.)

Currently the United States is the only wealthy, technologically sophisticated, medically advanced nation on earth that puts profits and money ahead of patients' best interests. We increasingly established this pattern of putting profit before patients in the decades following World War II, when all other Western nations were moving towards universal government-owned or -regulated healthcare. It is understandable, however, that we would have supported a capitalistic free market approach because we fervently believed that private capitalism would save money, drive efficiency, and improve quality. Unfortunately, we were wrong. Compared to all other advanced nations, it has not worked.

Many nations rank higher than the United States in healthcare. Because of their different cultural legacies and economic histories, all adopted a socialistic healthcare structure that considers patients interests and needs ahead of the quest for profits; this has worked better.

In my opinion, American healthcare will remain comparatively mediocre without ever attaining its full potential until we, too, put patients before profits.

As a previously uneducated believer that capitalism was the core *ism* for commerce, I was surprised when I finally came to this conclusion. I always try to keep space in my consciousness that I might be wrong, about anything. But after a number of years of reflection about this market aberration, I am increasingly confirmed that the free market does not always work well overall, but especially so in the healthcare economic sector.

Although better in many ways than the nonsystem of healthcare delivery that it substantially replaced, the Affordable Care Act perpetuates the money-before-people fatal flaw. It is based on allowing business interests to dominate the healthcare environment. Obamacare may be a bridge to the future, but if we really want the best for America, like Moses and Martin Luther King, it is not truly universal and most importantly, because of political compromise, remains profit-driven and will either be substantially reformed or replaced before we reach healthcare's promised land.

Approximately one-third of Americans now have either no insurance or insurance that is mostly useless. Surprisingly, most of American healthcare is already supported by tax dollars, in a sense already socialized. At this moment, to provide reasonable insurance for all Americans and achieve universal coverage that actually does put patients before profits, Medicare may turn out to be our best bet (see Chapter 7). Expanded Medicare would simply add to the approximately sixty-five percent socialization that already exists. After years of reading, writing, and discussion about our healthcare dilemma, it was actually a surprise when I concluded that Medicare for All, however long it might take to get here, would make a lot of sense. That's not where I began or what I expected.

"Listen" carefully as you continue reading and come to your own conclusions. We need to work together. We urgently need to be intelligent, not political. Whether or not Obamacare is repaired, if Medicare gains traction, or some other universal system becomes our choice, going forward I will use the term "Medicare" as my symbolic default label for any system of healthcare that is truly universal and people-driven, not profit-driven.

Finally, perhaps shockingly, perhaps erroneously, here's what I believe: Contrary to what you may have been told, if we adopt Medicare people will profit more and corporations less; it will save the majority of us a substantial amount of personal money and, if designed perspicaciously rather than politically, has the potential to save a substantial amount of money for our economy.

Earth provides enough to satisfy every man's needs, but not every man's greed.

– *Mahatma Gandhi*

Chapter 4
The Free Market: Healthcare's Secret Enemy

After writing *Assholistic Healthcare,* an earlier book about problems with our health system, I remained uncertain about the underlying cause of our mediocrity. When I began to think that the underlying problem was the free market – not the whole free market, just the market in healthcare specifically – I thought I might be nuts.

The path to universal, patient-driven, government-involved healthcare has long been suffocated by an intense devotion to the free market; we are attached to the idea that "the American way" must always embrace capitalism. For many of us, the free market is equivalent to the American flag, and nonsupport of free market solutions is equivalent to being unpatriotic.

For that reason, in the aftermath of World War II when other advanced wealthy nations focused more directly on patients' health interests, and chose some sort of government-regulated or -owned "socialistic" model, we essentially chose the free market as the captain and driver of our healthcare ship.

We had every reason to expect our supply and demand, market-based system to yield high quality healthcare at lower cost; but that's not what happened. Every other health-savvy sophisticated nation on earth has universal care, which we do not. We have also fallen well behind all other first-tier nations in measures of health, and we spend exponentially more money than anyone else.

Though I'm now in favor of Medicare, believing the free market in healthcare doesn't work and cannot be fixed, I still feel patriotic. I'm devoted to helping all Americans live longer and healthier lives with far fewer worries about healthcare. I don't want Americans to worry about a job they might not like, just to keep insurance. I don't want American business to have to add the burden of delving deep into the healthcare business at the expense of focus on their primary business, and then have the added economic burden of buying private insurance for all employees. I don't want Americans to feel the burden of spending more out of pocket on their healthcare than any other citizen group on earth. I don't want Americans to have to worry about bankruptcy due to medical bills when no other citizen group is so burdened. I also want to save the American economy substantial healthcare dollars (see Chapters 4 and 13).

Few people would suggest that the government must or should play a primary role in the auto industry, agriculture, home construction, the beauty industry, the computer industry, or the haberdashery business to name a few. But the failure of our market-driven healthcare model, in contrast with the relative healthcare success at lower cost of every other peer nation, is at least thought provoking.

I found some evidence to suggest that my idea

of a more virulent free market failure in healthcare was not completely insane. A great deal of academic economic literature has been written as though human beings were one more widget in the algorithm of market function; the implicit suggestion is that human economic behavior could be relied upon to be consistent – even robotic. Recently a few economists began to question that assumption.

In 2014, French economist Jean Tirole was awarded the Nobel Prize for explaining that the market could malfunction under certain circumstances (see *Economics for the Common Good).* Before Tirole, in 2002, psychologist Daniel Kahneman was awarded the Nobel Prize in Economics for his work with the late Amos Tversky on decision-making (see *Thinking Fast and Slow).* And recently, in 2017, economist Richard H. Thaler, considered the father of behavioral economics, was also awarded the Nobel in Economics for his substantial body of work making the point that sometimes people are systematically irrational (see *Nudge and Misbehaving).* Wearing my psychiatric hat, I had to smile and nod my head. Emotion and invisible fast thinking drives so much of life.

As I was writing this, President Biden's nominee for Treasury Secretary, previously the chair of the Council of Economic Advisors and the chair of the Federal Reserve, was confirmed. She is the first female Treasury secretary and the first person to have held all three positions. On November 27, 2020, economist Paul Krugman wrote an op-ed in *The New York Times* in which he noted that Dr. Yellin "... never forgot that economics is about people who aren't the emotionless, hyperrational calculating machines economists sometimes wish they were."

I believe the notion of market failure, in healthcare specifically, is something most legislators and pundits have probably never heard about; and if they have heard, it has been discounted or brushed aside as very difficult to believe. I've alluded to this, either explicitly or implicitly, in the introduction and many other chapters in which I promised to explain why the free market fails in healthcare. That time is now.

First, to a significant degree our health market is very complex, shrouded in an informational fog. When we (patients) want to make informed decisions about our care, it's difficult to really understand the quality of what we're buying, let alone the cost.

I'll use surgery as a healthcare example, although I do not intend to suggest that surgery has a more difficult set of problems. I could have chosen any area of medicine.

I had relatively minor surgery a few years ago, and I asked my doctor what his charge would be. He hesitated and said, "I have to do more operations than I used to in order to buy a car." I could sense that he may not have had an exact answer and that he was uncomfortable. I didn't push him.

I then asked him which of the hospitals he operated in had the lower infection rate. He again hesitated and said he thought the more local hospital did, but I wasn't sure that he really knew. I investigated and he was correct. (I wanted to minimize my risk of post-operative infection.)

I have practiced medicine in my community for a long time; I knew my doctor well, I respected him, and I knew other physicians felt the same. I probably had a deeper knowledge base than most members of the nonmedical community and therefore a better idea of what questions should be asked, but it would still have been more difficult to study my "purchase" of surgery than the way I could have studied the purchase of a new car or a new house.

Surgical quality is not entirely defined by a surgeon's rate of post-operative complications, or the number of similar surgeries that she has performed, or her success rate, but these are important aspects of due diligence. Try to find such information about your surgeon before your surgery. The information is usually known, but not always easy to come by.

On the cost front, did the doctor's charge or the hospital charge fit with the official description of that charge and your perception of the services? Did you even know to ask for that information? Did you know what your insurance would pay, assuming you had insurance, and what your financial obligation would be?

The ability and willingness of insurance companies, hospitals, physicians, pharmaceutical companies, and others to control, and perhaps even hide, information about cost and quality adds to the intrinsic complexity of healthcare purchasing. Your ability as a patient to get the best care at the best price is limited. The less you know, the more special interests have you over the proverbial barrel.

You would not buy a car without knowing the price; you would not rent a room in a hotel without knowing the price; you would not shop in a supermarket that did not display the price of merchandise. Yet every day in our healthcare supermarket, we purchase healthcare without knowing exactly what we are paying for, or how much we will be paying.

One myth is understandably and generally accepted by politicians and pundits about healthcare – again with some element of truth, but not as much as you might think. It goes something like this: If pricing were more transparent, people would seek the lower price and drive cost down. However, as you may have realized by now, many issues in healthcare are peculiarly abstruse and not at all what you would expect.

A June 26, 2019 article in *The New York Times* business section had the following headline: "Clear as Concrete: How Transparency Adds to Health Bill." In the article, Margot Sanger-Katz writes that "the peculiarities of the United States health care system, with its longstanding secrecy around negotiated health care prices, means there is very little research on the possible effect (of transparency)."

So far, a few studies done to see what effect transparency (cleaning the healthcare window) has on choice are a bit surprising. In many circumstances, transparency does not consistently lead patients to buy cheaper and, therefore, does not substantially reduce costs.

Undoubtedly, improving transparency could be a bit helpful. But it's not only cost that drives our decisions; and it's not always determined by insurance protection. If a lower cost item like a urinalysis is $35 at your local lab, but only $10 at a lab forty-five minutes away, you may still choose convenience.

Of immense importance in healthcare is the urgency of decision-making; time doesn't always allow for comparison shopping. Transparency is no less important, but damn near impossible, when you're in a medical rush. When you need care fast, you don't have time to ask many questions and do the due diligence.

You may not have thought of it this way: If you

currently have Medicare or Medicaid, the government has a far more transparent window to understand cost and value than we do as individuals. Medicare has in a sense already done extensive due diligence on your behalf, has already leveled the playing field by lowering cost and evening out some price differences; this saves both you and the economy a substantial amount of money. Thus, the government has appropriately restrained the constantly inflating, misfiring, dysfunctional healthcare "free" market.

In 1963, during discussions before the adoption of Medicare, Nobel winning economist Kenneth Arrow argued that healthcare insurance of any kind was problematic because it insulated the patient from direct financial responsibility and reduced incentive to look for the best deal. For example, if you have a choice between two labs and have private insurance, as Arrow suggested, you only have to pay part of the bill and there is less incentive to seek the better deal between two labs. You may not mind going to the higher-cost facility because you are protected by your insurance. This has some elements of truth (but with most insurance there are copays and deductibles, so we do have some skin in the game).

Arrow's concern further weakens when government insurance is involved. In that case, payment to the different labs would likely be the same, and the consequences of not looking for the best deal becomes moot.

Finally, some people are concerned that universal insurance protection would cause unnecessary excessive use of all medical facilities. Based on the experience from other lower cost, higher performing government insurance countries, patients don't flood doctors or facilities because they pay nothing or very little. Also, speculation is now that the enhancement of telemedicine, popularized during the pandemic, is quite likely to reduce most in-person use (and overuse) of emergency and perhaps other services.

Also, in the category of mythological misinformation is the continuing claim that allowing insurance competition across state lines would restrain pricing of insurance premiums. I believe this might be true for a very short time, but inevitably, as happened with the Obamacare insurance exchanges, after a few years of insurance company restraint, the quest for increased profit returned with a vengeance; premiums again began to rise and drive price inflation – surprise, surprise.

No matter what insurance you have, because of the way that the healthcare market works (or more accurately doesn't work), even with interstate competition you can be sure of only one thing – eventually (and it won't take long), all private insurance companies will raise your premium to maintain their profit margin because profit, not people, is the name of the game.

The bottom line is this: Healthcare is complex, multi-faceted, and multi-layered. And private insurance is so greedy that improving transparency or expanding competition is not as effective in lowering cost as it is in almost every other economic sector.

The core questions are these: Why is it that the free market doesn't work in healthcare? Why does informed government price regulation work in every other sophisticated wealthy nation on earth, keeping costs lower while healthcare performance is better overall?

The main reason the market doesn't work in the

health sector is very human and personal. The driving force, the core problem that sabotages free market function and turns the market into the "secret enemy" of healthcare is not a problem at all: *The market misfires because of the intrinsic personal value and elemental importance of health to each and every one of us.*

Without health, all life is diminished. Health is the river on which each and every life floats. Being healthy is a profoundly basic and important human value; it is why I so strongly suggest in Chapter 7 that healthcare is one of the services to which citizens of America or any other nation are truly entitled. It is the intensity of demand, our inherent human need for health, the depth of our desire to see that our children, our parents, and ourselves are as healthy as possible, that crushes and distorts usual free market function, rendering the market incapable of promoting quality while restraining cost.

Saying the same thing in a slightly different way, healthcare is so important that most of the time, no matter how many healthcare goods or services are provided, no matter how much supply is available, demand is almost never satisfied. If more is available, we want it. This anomaly has a name – it's called "inelastic demand."

Normally, if you manufacture too many automobiles, the market becomes saturated, the demand drops, and the price of cars drop. The same is true with apples, suits, houses, televisions, and just about everything else. It is *not* true about healthcare.

Unlike almost every other economic sector, the manufacturers of healthcare goods and services have entered an economic Magic Kingdom of sorts. For all intents and purposes, healthcare businesses can't lose. They're involved in a market sector that has a big gas pedal to push prices higher, but very undersized brakes to restrain costs. Put simply, competition does not work like it does in other sectors. The more doctors, hospitals, imaging centers, medications, and devices we produce, the more people buy. This is not absolute in every medical situation, but it is pervasive. This is not theory – it is fact.

Inelastic demand was demonstrated big time, right before our eyes during the coronavirus pandemic as we watched the price of N95 facemasks explode from $0.70 to $7.00 over the course of a few weeks. This is *profiteering*, and to some extent is what happens every day in the healthcare market. We patients, we human beings value healthcare so much that demand for healthcare goods and services is unrelenting. Cost inflation is chronic and unstoppable.

Every healthcare solution America has approached in the past few decades, including Obamacare, has been based on the delusion that economics in the health market works normally. Any attempt to fix American healthcare based on a free market capitalistic solution is doomed to continuing our healthcare mediocrity, at higher and higher prices, with less bang for the buck. No matter what, without government regulation, because the market misfires in healthcare, the gas pedal will constantly be pressed, insurance companies will seek more money, hospital costs will rise, pill costs will rise, doctors' fees will rise, and the cost of internal defibrillators will rise.

The brakes don't work. We've put money ahead of the patient's best interests, as we are patriotically nailed to a dysfunctional capitalistic environment in healthcare that while not perfect, is much more functional in other economic sectors.

As Americans, this notion of free market failure is hard to swallow. I do believe that a strong capitalistic free market produces better commercial efficiency than government regulation in almost all economic sectors. But peculiarly and anomalously, the government is better, more efficient, and more functional in healthcare.

What is the answer? A market-based healthcare solution is not the answer. My conclusion is not just theoretical. We have multiple examples of the success of non-market-based systems in healthcare. *Every other peer nation has a government-regulated healthcare system, every one of which works better overall, costs patients much less, and saves that country's economy a lot of money.*

Robert Lufrano and I are both former emergency physicians. I went on to practice psychiatry; he became the CEO of Blue Cross and Blue Shield of Florida from 2003 to 2011. We have discussed healthcare many times.

Blue Cross/Blue Shield of Florida is a massive health insurance company. It owns a subsidiary corporation that has a federal contract to administer approximately *one-third of all Medicare payments in the United States.* Bob said their administrative costs ran only 3 to 4 percent.

I had frequently seen figures of 4 to 6 percent for Medicare administrative costs, compared to 15 to 25 percent in the top-heavy and salary-heavy private sector. Thus, about ninety-five of every one hundred Medicare tax dollars goes directly to healthcare costs, while only seventy-five to eighty-five of one hundred private dollars go toward your healthcare.

I asked Dr. Lufrano what he thought was the best way to fix American healthcare. The former CEO of Blue Cross/Blue Shield replied simply, "Medicare."

"Can I quote you on that?"

"Absolutely."

I'm doing everything that I can, working with experts, really studying the statistics to figure out a way we can make it cool or normal to be kind and loving.

– *Lady Gaga*

Chapter 5
Numbers

If I told you that I was ranked number one in my medical school class, you might be impressed. If I then told you that I was the only member of the class, you would be less impressed. That additional information about class size is crucial and has the potential to drastically alter your opinion. This is often the case when we try to reach conclusions based on the statistics provided to us.

Mathematical and statistical information require close examination to interpret data fairly. Eventually, though, a picture begins to emerge. In the case of American healthcare, many have difficulty believing that our system is so mediocre relative to its potential. I hope to bring that picture into focus.

In 1991 and 2000, the World Health Organization (WHO) ranked healthcare based on three criteria that are each complicated:

- Improvement of health in a population, compared to what it might have been if there were no healthcare system at all

- Responsiveness of the system in terms of serving all citizens

- Fairness of financing between rich and poor, and the protection of citizens from financial loss due to serious illness

The WHO rankings of 191 nations, although much debated, continues to serve as a useful launch pad for discussion. You would probably not be surprised to learn that the United States ranked in the top 20 percent of the 191 countries whose healthcare systems were rated; but you probably would be surprised that we barely made that top fifth. Thirty-six countries had healthcare systems ranked ahead of us.

Our standing relative to other countries is most meaningful, however, when those other countries have sufficient wealth and population to make a fair comparison. Colloquially, we express this principle as apples-to-apples comparisons. Some say that 18 other nations are fair comparators. In a previous book, *Medicine's Moral Mess,* I took a conservative approach and selected only 13 of those 191 nations that were wealthy and populous enough to be fairly compared to the United States.

These comparators were all members of OECD, the Organization for Economic Cooperation and Development. A few examples of these nations in alphabetical order include Australia, Canada, France, South Korea, and the United Kingdom. (At the time, I didn't include Switzerland, Nordic nations, Israel, and many Middle Eastern countries that were wealthy enough and sophisticated enough, but their populations were smaller. Countries like China and

India certainly had the population but are developing and fragmented where healthcare is concerned.) The question was, where did we stand among this smaller number of peers?

The answer is that we fell below every one of those thirteen other nations. We were fourteenth, the bottom of the class. Despite our great wealth and advanced science, we were (and are) seriously underperforming.

I was repeatedly sensitized to this unhappy fact not only by reviewing statistics, but also by practicing medicine, by reading, by engaging in endless hours of discussion with interested individuals, and by reflecting on widely spaced visits to three of those thirteen OECD nations who performed better than we did. In 1967, during my senior year in medical school, I spent a month and a half studying in London. My sister-in-law lived in Paris many years ago, and we visited in 1982. In 2009, we spent time in Canada with friends.

London

It was twenty-two years after the end of World War II. *Star Trek* was making television history, and

Americans were two years away from walking on the moon. England has a government-owned or -regulated nonprofit universal healthcare system like every other industrialized country in the world – except us. Today, fifty years later, our "system" still does not provide universal coverage and as noted, it remains profit-driven and very expensive.

Beyond the formal medicine I learned in England, I formed two impressions that left me with a lot to think about. First and foremost, I felt that the medical practice of the English students and physicians with whom I worked did not seem in any way to be of lesser quality than that of their American counterparts. Second, even though financial pressures on American patients were not as severe as they are now, I felt envious of British patients who did not face financial worry if they became ill.

Some of my American medical colleagues who did most of their medical study in England are critical of the British socialized system. In part, this reflects their sometimes accurate perception that physicians make less money in England than in the U.S., and their variably accurate perception that access to care is more difficult in the British system. It is doubtful, however, that the millions of Americans with no health insurance, or inadequate health insurance, are better served than British citizens, all of whom have government-provided healthcare coverage.

Paris

In the winter of 1982, we traveled to Paris to visit my sister-in-law and her family. I asked Nancy about her experience with healthcare in France. Her summary was straightforward: "It's wonderful. The doctors are generally very good, it's relatively easy to make an appointment, and the cost is much lower than the United States."

Canada

We traveled with friends to Canada in the summer of 2009. I asked many of our Canadian neighbors about healthcare. The conversations went something like this: I would tactfully comment that some Americans believed that Canadian healthcare was "not great."

"No, it's very good," the Canadians would assure me.

"But don't you have to wait a long time for treatment?"

"Sometimes, and it can be aggravating, but if we need care urgently, we are treated immediately, and the care is excellent."

"Then why do so many people travel from Canada to the U.S. to get care?"

"I'm not sure how common that is, but most of the time it involves people who are well off financially and just don't want to wait."

Some Canadians told me something I found surprising: "I'll bet you don't know how many Americans living near the border find a Canadian address and come here for most of their care."

"But wouldn't you rather have the American system in Canada if you could?" I'd ask.

"No way!" I was told again and again. "Your healthcare costs are just ridiculous."

So how did we specifically stack up in the WHO rankings against these three OECD compatriots? Back then France ranked first in the world, England eighteenth, Canada thirtieth, and the United States thirty-seventh.

New information has emerged since those ratings. The Commonwealth Fund is a private foundation promoting improved healthcare, especially amongst those in the United States with lower incomes. For now, the World Healthcare Organization has stopped ranking nations, and it seems that the Commonwealth has partially taken up the gauntlet, choosing only eleven sophisticated nations that they consider to be comparable to the United States.

Many of the nations the Commonwealth Fund reported on in 2014 are amongst the OECD nations listed above, but they've dropped a few and added a few. The new list includes (in alphabetical order): Australia, Canada, France, Germany, the Netherlands, New Zealand, Norway, Sweden, Switzerland, the United Kingdom, and the United States. In their evaluation, the Commonwealth Fund incorporated some past data from both WHO and OECD.

The Commonwealth data attempts to be more nuanced than WHO and OECD. I believe it is. It includes five domains of healthcare: quality, access, efficiency, equity, and healthy lives. The data represents a more complex evaluation of fewer countries than the earlier World Health Organization rankings.

In reviewing this newer Commonwealth data, I'm going to focus primarily on the United States and the three nations I visited – England, France, and Canada. For those of you who are already apprehensive that we'll be overwhelmed with boring numbers, we're not going to travel in the deep weeds of the five health domains. Instead, I'll focus on a few salient details from each. (More comprehensive details can be googled under Commonwealth Fund, 2014 update entitled *"Mirror, Mirror on the Wall.")*

In the *quality* domain, out of eleven countries England is first, the United States fifth, France eighth, and Canada ninth.

Effective care includes preventive efforts. Here England is best, but the United States is relatively strong.

We also do well in assuring confidentiality, dignity, and promptness of care – attributes that go along with being patient-centered.

In terms of *access to care,* we're fairly far down at ninth. That low ranking is again because of cost-related issues. A huge swath of American patients can't afford to access care and don't seek help unless it's an absolute emergency. For those who can afford care, we're able to be timely with specialty care. But we do *not* have a sufficient number of primary physicians, and too many of us are driven to emergency care.

Since we're often told that we have better access than our Canadian friends, what's the real comparison? It turns out we are tied at ninth with Canada for access, but the issues are opposite. Remember that Canada has problems with providing timely elective specialty care and there are long waits. But they essentially have a Medicare-type system, and cost is not an issue.

By way of comparison, both England and France have enough primary care that emergency room use is much lower, and their overall costs are therefore lower. England ranks first in the efficiency category, France ranks eighth, and we rank eleventh. We spend way too much money, have too many administrative hassles for physicians, too much duplication of testing, and far too much avoidable emergency room use.

Equity is defined by the Institute of Medicine as "providing care that does not vary in quality because of personal characteristics such as gender, ethnicity, geographic location, and economic status." This is a more difficult category for the United States because we have more ethnic and geographic diversity than that of the other nations to which we are being compared. Low-income Americans were much less likely than low-income citizens of other nations to see a physician when sick, to fill a prescription, to get a recommended test, to go through treatment, or participate in follow-up care. We rank last.

The final domain is called *healthy lives* and is measured by studying three key indicators of overall health: infant mortality (we rank eleventh); healthy life expectancy (how much longer you will live if you arrive at age sixty in reasonable health – we rank tenth); and amenable mortality (we again rank eleventh).

For America, amenable mortality is a sad and provocative statistic. This is defined as "deaths per one hundred thousand patients under age seventy-five that could have been prevented with timely and effective care." France continues to rank first in this category as it has in the past.

According to amenable mortality, failures in France cause 65 deaths annually per 100,000 citizens, even with the best performing system. Though no system is ever likely to be perfect, our system (statistically) causes 110 deaths, 45 more per 100,000 population than our French allies. If our system performed as well as that of France, because of our larger population, we could estimate that our system would save about 125,000 more American lives per year than it does now.

The comparison I am about to make is in no way intended to diminish the poignant and tragic loss of life in the theatre of war. I honor and deeply appreciate the service and sacrifice of our military. Nor am I intending to be insensitive to the thousands of non-lethal injuries to American troops, or to the thousands of non-American injuries and deaths, whether military or civilian. However, the importance of improving the healthcare system in this country might be less appreciated without these numbers.

During fourteen years of war in Iraq and Afghanistan, we lost about 8,000 military men and women; also, as noted, many thousands more suffered life-changing injuries. However, during this same time frame, we theoretically lost as many as 1.6 million American patients because of correctable domestic healthcare system failures.

Through politically motivated TV ads and social media, we've often been misinformed about problems with other countries' healthcare. For instance, we're hammered that people in England and Canada have long waits for diagnostic procedures and elective treatments, resulting in loss of life. This is true. But given the approximately 125,000 Americans who may die annually because of inefficiencies in our own system, do the Canadians and British really wait any longer than our own underinsured (or uninsured) citizens who didn't even know they needed testing until it was far too late? According to the data from the Commonwealth Fund, the answer is no.

Some who resist universal healthcare might believe it costs less to insure fewer people. Counterintuitive though it might be, it does not lower cost to leave people uninsured; it actually costs more. Otis Webb Brawley made this poignantly clear in *How We Do Harm: A Doctor Breaks Ranks About Being Sick in America.* It is well known that continuity of care and preventive, proactive care are less expensive and more effective. We all pay for the exorbitant crisis-to-crisis healthcare costs of the uninsured.

So, how do we rank overall with the Commonwealth Eleven? We ranked thirty-seventh out of 191 countries with the WHO, behind all peer nations. We ranked fourteenth of fourteen in the OECD rankings. In this more recent Commonwealth Fund Study, it will be no surprise to find out that we rank eleventh overall of the eleven countries. One particularly blunt sentence in the Commonwealth report says it all: *The claim that the United States has the best healthcare system in the world is clearly not true.*

The value of improving our ranking in healthcare has nothing to do with bragging rights. It has to do with those 125,000 American patients who lose their lives each year. It has to do with an even larger number of Americans who lose quality of life, who can't work, or lose work time because of poor or absent medical care. Achieving a higher ranking translates into reducing the physical, emotional, and financial suffering of real people.

Finally, let's talk money – cold hard cash. What is the per capita expenditure on healthcare in the U.S. England, France and Canada? In 2018, the estimated per capita healthcare expenditure in the United States for every man, woman, and child averaged $10,209. Canada was next expensive at $6,839. Then comes France, at $4,902. Finally comes England at $4,264. Whose healthcare then ranked first and was highest in quality, lowest in cost? England.

More than 50 percent of bankruptcy in America is due to medical bills. There is controversy as to the actual number of yearly medical bankruptcies with estimates as high as more than 800,000 per year to as low as about 250,000 families per year. Whatever the actual figure, it is a large number. By way of contrast, how many families go bankrupt because of medical bills in England, France, and Canada? The answer is zero, zero, and zero.

Unfortunately, our COVID-19 pandemic has further unmasked fault lines; it has become a health-related financial missile attacking families and our economy. Would a better medical/public health response have led to less economic devastation? Probably, very likely, is the opinion of many wise men and women who understand healthcare and the economy. Would universal healthcare insurance have helped? Again, probably, very likely. Why?

First, the pandemic has been unmasking the already existing problems of America's dysfunctional healthcare. Millions of insurance disadvantaged Americans don't seek the care they might need because they have no insurance; more millions have such inadequate insurance that they, too, don't appropriately go to a doctor absent an absolutely raging medical problem.

Second, would a universal single-payer federal system have made it easier to mount a coordinated, efficient, scientifically-based nationwide public health response to the pandemic? Very likely.

Third, and less clear but related to the question above, would a coherent primary-payer universal insurance system have improved the medical community's ability to confront executive decisions that oppose medical science? Or put in a different way, *to better stand up to political decisions that were inappropriate from a public health perspective?* Maybe.

Fourth, governments responsible for the health of all of their citizens have a strong economic incentive to employ preventive medicine to promote public health.

In his book *The Healing of America,* author T.R. Reid interviews John Reid, then chief of the British National Health Service, who explains why his prevention program is more robust than the United States; healthier citizens save the government a lot of money (see Chapter 13).

Contrast that to the U.S. where private insurance seems less incentivized to promote health in this way.

In the June 2020 issue of *The New Republic,* Alexander Zaitchik's "No Vaccine in Sight: The U.S. Was Once at the Cutting Edge of Pandemic Prevention. Then Big Pharma Took Over" offers this relevant excerpt:

> "The scarcity of more complicated tools to address a catastrophic public health crisis – including ventilator machines, other medical devices, and, most elusive of all, a vaccine – doesn't have such simple state-level answers. But these shortages do raise a similar set of questions: about the patent system, about pandemic preparedness policy, about the value of a private health sector structurally incapable of prioritizing high-risk

low-probability events."

At the very least, there is understandable context to all three areas of public health concern with our hybrid, nonuniversal American system.

If we already had universal health insurance in America, would we now be better off in these pandemic times? I don't know. If we already had universal health insurance in America, is it *possible* that we would be better off? Yes!

I am not clairvoyant, but I sincerely believe that universal health insurance, in the U.S. probably Medicare, is worth a shot. When it comes to a pandemic, in terms of human cost and dollar cost, an ounce of prevention is not worth a pound of cure, it's worth a thousand pounds of cure.

I don't make jokes. I just watch the government and report the facts.

– *Will Rogers*

Chapter 6
The Affordable Care Act: Obamacare

At this moment, the future of our healthcare remains uncertain. The best of American medicine is excellent, but we have developed what must be defined as one of the most fragmented and dysfunctional healthcare delivery systems among comparable wealthy nations. Too many Americans never get our best.

The past decade of healthcare evolution has been dominated by Obamacare turbulence. Now, finally gaining traction, over the next ten years it is likely to undergo modification and may even disappear.

Having witnessed the perturbations of the Obamacare era, often stirred and intoxicated by hostile forces, I feel special annoyance awards are due our politicians and pundits who make broad sweeping, inaccurate statements misinforming us about our healthcare in general and, flawed as it may be, about Obamacare specifically.

We are sometimes advised that we already have universal healthcare because we all are able to receive care in an emergency room. Hogwash! I practiced emergency medicine for thirteen years. It is profoundly expensive and not remotely equivalent to having good health insurance.

We are also told that we have the best healthcare in the world – possibly true for those who have great access, but definitely not true for a large swath of patients who don't. This represents about a third of our fellow Americans.

We are told that people die in Canada and England because they don't have the access to healthcare that we do. There are instances when this is true, but we are *not* told that by far, more people die in the United

States than in Canada or England because of the lack of adequate insurance and delays in our system.

A few years back I labeled our pre-Obamacare era as the *Assholistic Healthcare* era – a dysfunctional medical hodgepodge built upon a foundation of accumulated mistakes. Obamacare is an improvement, though not an ultimate solution. With the unfair benefit of hindsight, here are a few examples of the mistakes that the ACA perpetuates, the two most important of which are:

- The choice *not* to implement universal healthcare after World War II

- The choice to build a healthcare system upon the premise that our guide should be market mechanisms dependent upon money making and profit taking, instead of what's in the best interest of patients

As we move forward, some act as though these mistakes are sacrosanct and must be preserved. But if we consider what's best for patients – you and me, our children, parents, and friends – this is idiocy.

I do not lay claim to be one of the few people who know every nook and cranny of this more than two-thousand-page Affordable Care Act (ACA or Obamacare, as it's familiarly known). Given what I do know and in light of the dysfunctional partisan political terrain we have today, the ACA is a remarkably intelligent piece of legislative complexity. Despite deficiencies, I appreciatively reflect that Obamacare has benefitted far more people than those whose health situations were made worse.

Somehow in its legislative maze of corridors, Obamacare managed to improve the lot of many patients, and initially appease the money hunger of the special interests sufficiently to allow support for passage of the bill.

Obamacare has enlightened the public about the importance of the pre-existing condition exclusion and caps (limits) on the amount of coverage we can have in a given period of time.

Obamacare also allowed young adults to remain on their parents' insurance to age twenty-six. Such benefits do make insurance coverage more reliable and financially protective.

Overall, in part because of some expansion of Medicaid and because financial subsidies supported many patients who bought private insurance, about twenty-four million more people ended up with insurance than had been the case during the preceding era of Assholistic care.

Despite these benefits, however, the healthcare scene represented by Obamacare will probably never achieve full universal coverage, and will continue to support healthcare with an inevitably expensive market-based, profit-driven system in which business entities, primarily motivated by money, often tell doctors what they can and cannot do for patients. By allowing the "profit before people" philosophy to continue, Obamacare, like the Assholistic system before it, feeds into this unfairness.

In Obamacare, the original mechanism to broaden the base of insured Americans was the mandate that everyone purchase health insurance, often with government help, or pay a fine. The mandate did expand the number of insured individuals but would probably never have led to full universal coverage, even had it remained in place.

As I watched the cacophony of the state-by-state decisions about the constitutionality of mandated insurance, or acceptance of Medicaid, I was not surprised. In law school I came to understand that our body of law is not as solid, rigid, or definite as many believe – nor is it predictable.

Law is significantly and inevitably influenced by prevailing cultural trends, especially involving psychology, sociology, and even politics. Although the legal speed limit, which is "law," remains the same on any given road, not everyone stopped for exceeding, say, fifty-five miles per hour will be ticketed. Nine Supreme Court justices, when faced with the same case, the same legal briefs, the same oral arguments, and the same "elephant" will all see that elephant a little differently.

The Affordable Care Act is clearly a compromise, forged in the crucible of political intransigence and special interest dominance. I detest the partisan Obamacare bickering that went on after its passage and is perhaps beginning to dissipate. It is not the final solution, but it's simply not the disaster that's been described. It may be an adequate bridge to a future of excellence, but as you will come to understand, it is not the promised land. Perhaps there are ways to "repair and improve" instead of "repeal and replace" Obamacare, but ultimately, as long as profit is put ahead of patients' best interests, neither a repaired Obamacare nor any form of market-dominated healthcare will ever work very well. In America today, given our many advantages, there is absolutely no reason *any* American should have to tolerate mediocrity and astronomical expense where healthcare is concerned.

> Prejudice is a burden that confuses the past, threatens the future and renders the present inaccessible.
>
> – *Maya Angelou*

Chapter 7
Socialism and Other Dirty Words

We are all limited to our perspective, and why not? Each of us has a personal reality that reflects the impact of family, cultural experience, social relationships, geography, political environment, and especially genetic makeup. Although we are not prisoners of our biology by any means, there is an undeniable genetic nudge that inhabits us always (see Chapter 1).

We are each so wedded to our belief system and view of life that any departure from it, be it a change of mind or perspective, feels like a rip in the fabric of our existence. I try to be objective, but I am aware that my own subjectivity is always there. I can only present my perspective that you then filter through your perspective. This inevitable personalization leads all of us to subconsciously have a slant on everything we think and hear.

Often, ironically, I see situations in which someone inadvertently and inexorably takes a position that actually runs counter to their own personal, financial, and medical self-interest. As the saying goes, this is like shooting yourself in the foot. I'm sure I've done it plenty of times.

There was a joke circulating on the internet during the early Obamacare years that was a spoof on human subjectivity:

> The American Medical Association has weighed in on the new Obama healthcare proposals. The allergists voted to scratch it, but the dermatologists advised not to make any rash moves. The gastroenterologists had sort of a gut feeling about it, but the neurologists thought the

Administration had a lot of nerve. The obstetricians felt they were all laboring under a misconception. Ophthalmologists thought the idea shortsighted. Pathologists yelled, "Over my dead body!" While the pediatricians said, "Oh grow up!"

The psychiatrists thought the whole idea was madness, while the radiologists could see right through it. Surgeons decided to wash their hands of the whole thing. The internists thought it was a bitter pill to swallow, and the plastic surgeons said, "This puts a whole new face on the matter." The podiatrists thought it was a step forward, but the urologists were pissed off at the whole idea. The anesthesiologists thought the whole idea was a gas, and the cardiologists didn't have the heart to say no. In the end the proctologists won out, leaving the whole thing up to the assholes in Washington.

In preparation for reading the rest of *Patients Before Profits* I ask that you give some extra consideration to the following words: socialism, entitlement, rationing.

Socialism

Most of us think of America as a beehive of capitalism. This is true, but much of America's financial honey is really a hybrid, blending capitalism and socialism. Although it is not easy for some to accept, the *isms* are complementary financial/social structures – not mutually exclusive. From the beginning they shared the stage.

Look at our American world with fresh eyes. The U.S. Postal Service is socialized, but the trucks the postal service purchases are products of private industry. Private contractors supply stone and steel for government projects. Equipment used by army physicians (socialized medicine) is usually manufactured by private industry.

For a while we've been mired in the middle of a bitter battle between those who strongly prefer private enterprise and those who are tolerant of greater government involvement. Neither capitalism (private ownership or control) nor socialism (government ownership or control) is simply good or bad. Neither the private sector nor the government is a center of efficiency or morality, nor is either the total or even the dominant provider of necessary goods and services in American life.

Some would say that unless something is wholly government-owned it is not socialized. For instance, the Veterans Administration could be considered socialized, while Medicare might not fit the more rigorous definition. *The American Heritage Dictionary of the English Language* simply defines socialized as "something that is placed under government or group ownership or control."

Our educational system is blended – a hybrid of socialized public schools, semi-socialized (publicly-funded) charter schools, private parochial schools, and private nonreligious institutions. All schools, socialized or not, require support (services and supplies) from private industry.

Infrastructure is blended; both government and private entities that build our roads, bridges, waterways, electrical grids, and cyber networks all reflect some combination of our two main *isms*. All who build and maintain infrastructure purchase goods and services from private businesses. Without our infrastructure, whether born of hybrid, government or private projects, our entire system of commerce would implode.

Safety services are for the most part socialized; they are not free and are paid for mostly by taxes. We don't receive a personal bill each time we use police or fire protection, or when our military or national guard acts to keep us safe. Unlike health, we have accepted a sort of universal socialized safety insurance. Safety services (police, fire, military, national guard) are much more like Medicare than our current health system. Despite this "safety socialism" in our primarily capitalistic nation, we have historically had blinders on where healthcare is concerned. In my opinion, safety would be just as dysfunctional as our current health system if we ran it like health – not just dumb, but dangerous.

Why is that? It is because, like health, the regard for the safety of our families and our nation is a profound human value, too important to be left to the uncertainties of the free market. Imagine if you dialed "911" and the operator asked, "Does your police or fire insurance cover emergencies?"

Safety and health involve values that embrace

mankind's ability to grow and sustain civilization. Every competent government the world over provides some universal socialized safety services. Every competent government *except the United States* provides a version of universal socialized healthcare system that covers their citizens' medical needs without undue financial burden.

Although we don't yet provide universal socialized healthcare insurance, a lot more of American healthcare than you might realize is already socialized. Medicare, Medicaid, military medicine, most prison medicine, the Veterans Administration, the Indian Health Service, services of the CDC (Communicable Disease Center), and many medical departments of state universities are socialized.

By 2016, according to the *American Journal of Public Health,* tax dollars were already funding nearly two-thirds of American healthcare, 64.3 percent to be exact. *Webster's College Dictionary* defines tax as "a sum of money levied on income, property, sales, etc., by a government for its financial support or specific services." Essentially, taxation is a constitutionally approved system of income redistribution.

And if I were foolish enough to expose the socialism that is never identified as such, but is hiding under a gargantuan American rug, what might we find? That the income from ordinary people has been vastly redistributed to the oil industry and agriculture. Does this sufficiently qualify these large businesses as participating in American hybrid socialism? I don't think so, but it's an interesting question.

I point this out not to criticize or support any socialistic American industry. I'm simply making an observation that most Americans are blind to the socialism that's all around us. The irony is that most of these socialistic operations were conceived of or approved by a Congress who markets itself as anti-socialistic. What hypocrisy.

I believe our Founding Fathers structurally included the ability to tax in our Constitution to establish a system by which we could care for our needs and some needs of the less fortunate, thus redistributing income by sharing some of our wealth. Remember, at the Boston Tea Party we objected not to taxation, but "taxation without representation."

Some taxes are hidden by not using the word tax. In this ongoing healthcare debate, one ironic hidden tax is employer-based health insurance. When an employer pays for part or all of your healthcare premiums, you are automatically taxed because the money the employer provides for your insurance usually reduces the actual dollar wage you receive.

Many Americans believe in the concept of taxation to some degree. But there is a constant debate about the particular use of tax, inefficient use of tax dollars, and our complex tax laws. Paul Volker, Chairman of the Federal Reserve Board under Ronald Regan, once described our particular tax system as evidence for aliens that this planet did not support intelligent life.

Our tax system needs overhauling, but taxation as a method of sharing, helping, and protecting is just as relevant today as it was in 1788 when the Constitution was ratified.

Healthcare reform suffers if the focus becomes an intransigent philosophic battle between those who prefer private enterprise and those who prefer more government involvement. As noted, in healthcare (as with safety, infrastructure, and education) we already have systems that are both capitalistic and socialistic. Neither is simply good or bad; both are a mixed bag.

The government imperfectly supports our constitutionally guaranteed rights to life, liberty, and the pursuit of happiness by providing goods and services that we as a culture believe are important and, for various reasons, cannot be provided as well by private enterprise alone. The private sector imperfectly supports our constitutionally guaranteed rights to life, liberty and the pursuit of happiness by providing goods and services that we as a culture believe are important and, for various reasons, cannot be provided as well by the government. The derogatory and oversimplified mantra of "government bad, private good" is partisan, powerful, and provocative. This mantra contributes to the perpetuation of our creaking, groaning, cost-bloated, dysfunctional healthcare nonsystem that is in urgent need of repair.

Prior to and during the Cold War, the concept of socialism was linked to a hostile communistic totalitarian past. This evil conception of socialism is carried forward as an echo of history, refreshed by current abuses in Venezuela and encouraged for partisan political purposes. I believe this kind of association is profoundly inappropriate in modern America.

We in the United States, despite recent partisan rhetoric, are not moving toward socialism; to a substancial degree we're already there. The hybrid American socialism that now exists has been thriving for decades. It does not resemble the evils of Russia or Germany or Venezuela; nor does it exactly mimic the sunnier and more generous vision of Norway, Sweden, and Denmark.

As we, of necessity, sculpt our own vision for the healing of our current partisan explosion and hopefully the ascension of intelligence over political sausage, I believe America will continue to be a positive, creative, and innovative pioneer of government and democracy, including creative and innovative economic "ism" hybrid.

Entitlement

A few years ago, a friend and writer said to me, "The difference between a good word and the exact word is the difference between a lightning bug and lightning." Words and their meaning are important. One word that I've thought about a great deal is "entitlement" or, more specifically, the political use of this word in the United States.

To be entitled to something is to have proper grounds for claiming it. Thus, an entitlement is something you actually deserve, not something you actually don't deserve. Yet in America, more than a hint of condescension and unworthiness accompanies the political use of the word entitlement. It is sort of a cynical value judgment that what someone is receiving is to some degree a giveaway that a government should not really have to provide.

Instead of automatically going along with the politically distorted implication of this word, what if we were to evaluate our entitlements according to the accurate definition? Let's think of entitlements in their native environment, without the political distortion, as something you really deserve, not something you really don't deserve.

We can now ask three very cogent and meaningful questions: What is it to which we are really entitled from a government that is competent? What is it that government is well suited to provide, either alone or with the private sector, that would be unavailable from the private sector alone? And, bottom line, Why bother to have a government in the first place?

In answering this question, I focused on what is needed at a very minimum to pursue American values of life, liberty, and happiness. Although government provides many helpful services, my answer did not include infrastructure, scientific and medical research, social security, welfare, national parks, environmental services, agricultural support, food stamps, or government grants. You may argue that some of these programs are valuable and desirable and might be included in your list. I was sticking to what I consider absolutely core needs.

Being very careful and conservative, in order to justify the existence of a government, I include only four basic entitlements:

1) A System of Law – Without this, despite the imperfections of all legal systems, why bother having a government? Chaos does not lend itself to civilization. In the context of what is possible in an individual life, how do you predictably pursue life and liberty, and how are you able to maximize happiness without some system of law, like a Constitution?

2) Health – If you don't have your health, life itself is diminished. If you don't have your health, you can have all the wealth and beauty in the world and be miserable. If you're sick, it doesn't matter much what kind of car you drive, whether General Motors fails, how well Amazon or Apple are doing, or the size of your living room. Medicare, anyone?

3) Safety – In the context of what is possible in an individual life, how do you pursue life and liberty, and how are you able to maximize happiness if you and your family are not safe (or healthy)? Think police, fire, military, etc.

4) Education – Especially in an age of rapid change, modern society and commerce would implode without a foundation of at least basic literacy and practical training for all Americans.

Without laws, health, safety, and educational services, everything we hold dear, everything we value, everything we do is diminished. In the context of what is possible in an individual life, how do you pursue life and liberty, and how are you able to maximize happiness without these *real* entitlements?

Government cannot provide perfect legal or educational systems; nor can it guarantee your health or safety at every moment. However, by imperfectly providing these essential services, it lays the foundation for everyone to live reasonably and have a better shot at making the most of their existence.

Ironically, the only so-called entitlements that politicians refer to as entitlements that actually deserve to be called entitlements *are* health related, especially Medicare and Medicaid. Those other snide, condescending, politically-described entitlements, like welfare and social security, are not slam-dunk entitlements at all; perhaps they should or deserve to be labeled "compassionate services," bestowed by a benevolent society through its government.

Whatever description suits you, as a society the current distortion of the word entitlement profoundly influences perspective.

Some folks who do regard healthcare as a privilege, a more non-entitled entitlement, likely feel that those who don't provide for their health are somehow lazy, leeches, or loafers. Perhaps some individuals fit those characterizations, but most don't. (Be reminded what Dr. Alan Halperin had to say about his university practice in Chapter 2.)

I've sometimes asked financially successful friends, who feel they don't want to pay for those who somehow haven't "pulled their weight" or are "cheaters," the following questions:

Should we be denying help for those who are truly less fortunate?

No, is the usual response; however, it is occasionally yes.

Would you want to change places with those who you think don't deserve our help and are gaming the system?

No, is always the response.

Would your life be diminished in any significant way if you had a few less dollars?

That's not the point – it's the principle, is a common answer.

What sort of "principle" leads some men toward not wanting to pay extra for insurance that covers pregnancy because "I'm never going to be pregnant"? Funny, I never hear women complain about paying extra for our prostate problems.

We can't eliminate human nature. There will always be those of us who are inclined to be more or less generous or charitable. Whether or not I personally agree with someone, in a democracy we don't expect everyone to have the same opinion. In fact, democracy is all about disagreement. I always try to understand and be respectful.

I also understand that there will always be some people who try to cheat or game the system, any system, and they should be dealt with. But I have never felt that any small contribution I've made to the well-being of others, whether through tax I've paid, charitable contributions, pro-bono work, or participation in the general stream of commerce (even if some of it inevitably trickles to gamers), has diminished the quality of my life in any way – quite the contrary. But I can understand and respect the feelings of those who disagree.

Having universal healthcare does not necessarily require a primary/single-payer system or a socialized system; it simply means that everyone has coverage. However, realistically and as far as I can tell, all systems that provide universal coverage are to a substantial degree socialized.

Perhaps in the process of discussing, debating, and developing universal healthcare, likely Medicare, we can find a way to recover that graceful human value of compassion that our Founding Fathers so robustly supported, at least in spirit .

The United States has never had universal healthcare, not even close.

In the November 2, 2009, edition of Newsweek magazine, Anna Quindlan wrote the following healthcare-related article entitled "Hope Springs Eternal":

"Universal healthcare is the area in which the

gap between what's needed and what's likely is most glaring, and the limitations of the president's power most apparent. It is dispiriting to watch the cheerleaders of American exceptionalism pound their chests and insist that our citizens do not need the kind of system that virtually every other developed nation finds workable.

As elected officials posture and temporize, families are bankrupted by healthcare costs and forgo treatment they can't afford. Statistical measures of national health, from life expectancy to infant mortality continue to be substandard.

And because we have that system of checks and balances, in which movement usually happens slowly and sporadically, a great need for sweeping reform may be met with a jury-rigged bill neither sufficiently deep or broad, which perhaps someday will give way to a better one, and then eventually a truly good one."

Rationing

This dirty word has been so overhyped and

politicized, that public fearfulness borders on the irrational.

"Here Come the Death Panels" is an op-ed written by Michelle Goldberg that appeared in *The New York Times* on March 24, 2020. The following is part of what she had to say:

> "We were told that if America passed Obamacare, it would result in death panels. This lie was invented by Sarah Palin in 2009, during the fight for what would become the Affordable Care Act. It was the hysterical version of the common conservative critique that universal health care means government rationing. …The argument was always specious, but it looks especially absurd in light of the coronavirus tearing through the world. America's inadequate healthcare system far from increasing liberty, is poised to make death panels more likely.
>
> As waves of sick people crash onto undersupplied hospitals, doctors are preparing to make choices about who will get access to ventilators and other equipment, and who will get only palliative care…"

If private insurance companies, whether for profit or nonprofit, or government insurance won't pay for certain medical procedures such as MRIs or CAT scans, *we are rationing.* If we allow some Americans to go without any healthcare coverage, Americans who may not have the financial means to purchase private healthcare insurance, *we are rationing.*

The list could go on and on. Every private medical insurance company rations healthcare. Every government medical insurance program, including Medicare, rations healthcare. Any healthcare plan you personally favor will include rationing. To ration is "to restrict something to a limited allotment." It would be relatively easy to design healthcare reform if we had the money to provide anything and everything we needed. But we don't, and we never will. *Every nation on the face of this earth, including the United States, has healthcare rationing.*

Over the years of my practice, most of my insurance aggravation seemed to come from the private side. Medicare presented some frustrations, more for the physician than the patient; but private insurance companies seemed far more restrictive in approaching requests for actual patient care. Was my impression correct? I never studied it explicitly, so I'm not sure. Might I have been correct? Absolutely.

As we develop a better healthcare system, we should be mindful of the Hippocratic ideal of placing patients' best interests above all other concerns – but this is possible only to the extent our financial means permit. We will not be able to serve the best interest of each patient in every case. However, protecting the best interests of patients and cutting costs are not mutually exclusive goals; indeed, quite the opposite is true. Together the two goals can lead to a much wiser use of money.

Rationing is not a zero-sum game where gains and losses offset one another exactly. It is possible for rationing to result in a net gain or a net loss of value. When we choose something of greater value and eliminate something of lesser value, we are *value adding*. Thoughtful rationing requires that we identify and prioritize what we value, and intentionally add value. Otherwise, thoughtless or uninformed rationing is likely to produce net losses.

Honestly, what we should include or exclude

will never be entirely settled. But the continuous process of making choices may, through experience and thoughtful reflection, become increasingly sophisticated.

Twenty-seven years ago, Dr. John Kitzhaber, an emergency physician and then governor of Oregon, guided the development of a state healthcare rationing plan based on presumably reasonable projections of the scope, intensity, and costs of different medical diagnoses. Kitzhaber's plan was initially unsuccessful, in part because even the notion of rationing was too bitter a political pill. But it was one of the first major state-guided efforts at healthcare reform.

Eventually, some aspects of his plan were adopted, and until the 2008 economic downturn, Oregon was successfully reducing the number of its uninsured residents. After a lengthy absence, Kitzhaber was reelected governor of Oregon on November 2, 2010, but resigned after a relatively short time in office.

I heard Dr. Kitzhaber speak in Monterey, California in October 1992, while he was governor. He was kind enough to send me a copy of his healthcare plan and the text of the speech he delivered that day. With his permission, I want to share an excerpt of that eloquence with you:

"As most of you know, the Bush administration (George H.W. Bush) in August denied Oregon's Medicaid waiver request preventing us (for the time being) from extending basic healthcare services to over 400,000 Oregonians who are currently excluded from the system. But we haven't given up – not by a long shot. And to try to understand why I have engaged this issue so vigorously, and continue to do so, let me share with you an experience I had almost twenty years ago that helped to shape my thinking on these matters.

In the fall of 1973, at the very beginning of my internship, I watched a baby die – a little boy weighing less than three pounds whose name was Sam. His mother was poor; and as she had not once seen a physician during her pregnancy, she was seriously anemic. Sam was born prematurely in the emergency room, then transferred to the neonatal intensive care unit, where he died two days later.

I can still remember standing by his incubator

during that final hour, knowing what was going to happen and feeling depressed and helpless. I remember what a quiet death it was. It never made the papers or the evening news, so no one really knew about Sam's two-day struggle to live. No one was there at the end except Sam's parents, a nurse, and me. It was an anonymous tragedy, touching the lives of no one but those in the room.

A day or two after Sam died, I witnessed another death that I still vividly remember as that of a ninety-year old woman with lung cancer whose name was Gladys. She had gone into cardiac arrest following surgery to remove her right lung, surgery she hadn't really wanted, but her family insisted.

When the code was called on the surgery floor, I rushed to the room along with another intern, a surgical resident, two nurses, and a respiratory therapist. The six of us spent an hour in a frantic but unsuccessful attempt to save her.

Her final hour, unlike baby Sam's, was far from quiet. We stuck tubes in her nose, her throat, her bladder. We stuck needles into her veins, we pumped her full of drugs, and shocked her repeatedly. Yet we "failed." She died and ran up a posthumous bill of thousands to be picked up by her family or her estate.

I have remembered these two people, I think, because death was still new to me then, and because they both died on my shift. I also remembered the curious contrast between the frenzied efforts of a room full of people with all their sophisticated equipment, to save someone at the very end of a long life and the quiet and undramatic death of someone at the very beginning of life.

Sam died because we didn't know as much then as we do now about respiratory distress syndrome in newborns. But he also died because somehow nobody had made the token investment to get this mother the prenatal care that would have prevented his prematurity and low birth weight.

Gladys died because she was ready to die. She recognized that, but her family couldn't. Nor could we. We had been trained to view death as a failure, not a natural part of the life process. We never stopped to consider whether trying to resuscitate her made sense – whether the costs in dollars and suffering was really compassionate given her underlying diagnosis of terminal lung cancer.

Certainly it never occurred to me then to connect the money spent on her final hour with the money not spent on Sam during his mother's pregnancy. Twelve years later, however, my recollection of these events would take on a new significance, and I would see them as proof that implicit legislative policy choices affect human lives in ways that policymakers do not always foresee.

No one explicitly chose to deny care to Sam's mother; yet a choice in favor of, say, heroic measures for the terminally ill amount to an implicit choice against some other kinds of care, such as the care that might have allowed Sam to live. This is an important point, and it lies at the heart of the Oregon Health Plan: in a world of fiscal limits, a reality which Oregon has confronted head-on, an explicit choice to fund one set of services is always at the same time an implicit choice not to fund something else."

As Governor Kitzhaber implied, Gladys was

inevitably dying. Nothing anyone could possibly have done would have saved her. Had she been treated with compassion and focus on her comfort, she would have passed away comfortably.

In today's world she might have had a living will. In 1973, it is likely she did not. Regardless, to have allowed her to die with dignity is in no way "the action of inducing the painless death of a person for reasons assumed to be merciful," which is the definition of euthanasia.

No current or pending reform plans include anything that resembles euthanasia, or those so-called death panels, but there were people who were absolutely determined to interpret it that way. As stated earlier, "It's not what you say to someone, it's what they hear."

There will always be differences of opinion about specific rationing strategies. Adding value will always require medical science, intention, due diligence, and a persistent willingness to learn from experience.

Until the Affordable Care Act, any sign of possibly significant illness would likely have triggered the profit-driven pre-existing condition clause once the insurance was up for renewal. The premium could then skyrocket, or previously-insured individuals could be denied coverage by their insurance company. This is rationing of the worst kind, diverting resources from people most in need in order to protect a wider profit margin.

Again, rationing exists and will continue to exist until everyone has enough of everything to fulfill every need.

That day will never arrive, no matter how wishfully you desire it or how fervently you deplore limitation.

No matter what healthcare system we eventually have in America, we sorely need value-driven, rational rationing that reduces cost while improving overall care, and that means acknowledging some of the irrational rationing that we now have.

Part II
Money Matters

When I told my doctor I couldn't afford an operation, he offered to touch-up my X-rays.

– Henny Youngman

Chapter 8
The Medical Profession

Dr. Ezekiel Emanuel is a highly regarded oncologist and bioethicist, who serves as Vice Provost for Global Initiatives and chair of the Department of Medical Ethics and Health Policy at the University of Pennsylvania. In June 2020, he published his fourteenth book, *Which Country Has the World's Best Health Care?* This book is our previous Chapter 4 on steroids. I strongly recommend it if you're interested in expanding on the subject. (And I also suggest one of his earlier books listed in my bibliography.)

I've had great respect for Dr. Emanuel's thinking and expertise, which is why I was compelled to review his new book – published a few months before the completion of *Patients Before Profits.* Although we were generally on the same page, we absolutely agreed that the United States does not have the best healthcare in the world.

In addition to the relevance of *Which Country has the World's Best Health Care?,* I was serendipitously intrigued by a comment made by Peter Osnos, founder of Public Affairs and publisher of Dr. Emanuel's book:

> "Public Affairs is a publishing house founded in 1997. It is a tribute to the standards, values, and flair of three persons who have served as mentors to countless reporters, writers, editors, and book people of all kinds, including me."

Two of the three were Ben Bradlee, longtime editor of *The Washington Post,* and Robert Bernstein, longtime chief executive of the major publisher, Random House. What caught my attention, however, was the third icon, I.F. Stone.

While investigating the medical profession's relationship to market-based healthcare back in the 1940s, I was surprised to run into a distant cousin. My great-grandfather was the oldest of seven brothers who immigrated to the United States from Russia around the turn of the twentieth century. My grandmother, Sadie Feinstein, was one of his children. Isidore Feinstein was a son of the youngest of the seven brothers; although he was my grandmother's first cousin, she was much older. My mother, Izzie's first cousin once removed, was his contemporary and they knew each other well.

Isidore Feinstein grew up to be I.F. Stone, a respected journalist in the mid-twentieth century. However, Senator Joe McCarthy eventually accused him of being a communist and had him blackballed.

In all fairness, I.F. Stone was an intellectual gadfly and provocateur. Often seemingly outrageous, the years have tended to confirm much of his writing; he was uncannily accurate and ahead of his time.

I.F. was frequently on radio and TV and worked as a correspondent for *The Nation* and for *PM,* described as a "legendary New York tabloid that refused advertisements and revolutionized American newspapers." His downhill slide apparently began in 1950 while speaking at a rally denouncing the hydrogen bomb. This is how he began his comments: "FBI agents and fellow subversives." That really pissed off a few important people.

By the time of that rally, he had written four successful books. After that, no one would publish his fifth book about the Korean War. He was forty-four years old and could get no work. Connecting with some of his devoted readers he launched his own newspaper, *The I.F. Stone Weekly.* As a teenager I was a subscriber. He developed a substantial readership and was able to put food on the table. Eventually, his career was resurrected.

I began to browse his biography, *American Radical: The Life and Times of I.F. Stone* by D.D. Guttenplan, not with the expectation that I would find material relevant to *Patients Before Profits,* but simply out of curiosity. Suddenly I was reading information that spoke to our current healthcare tumult. The following is from the introduction of Guttenplan's book:

"To the Meet the Press audience on December 12, 1949, there was nothing special about the confrontation between I.F. Stone and Dr. Morris Fishbein. As editor of the *Journal of the American Medical Association,* Fishbein was a well-known foe of what the AMA called "socialized medicine" in any form; Stone, a sometime member of the Meet the Press panel since 1947, could always be relied on for provocative, irreverent, and persistent questioning.

The country's most influential physician had already denounced national health insurance as "the kind of regimentation that led to totalitarianism in Germany." When Fishbein also condemned compulsory coverage as "socialistic," Stone demonstrated why the show's producers considered him "a good needler": 'Dr. Fishbein, let's get nice and rough. In his advocacy of compulsory health insurance, do you regard Mr. Harry Truman as a card-bearing communist or just a deluded fellow traveler?'"

In 1964, fifteen years after the Stone-Fishbein *Meet the Press* episode, and two years before the United

States adopted Medicare, I began medical school. It was my perception when I entered medical school that I was becoming a part of the medical "profession." Certainly, if I ever went out on my own as a private practitioner, I would be running a small business (something I knew nothing about), but it was not my primary concern. I believe the same could be said at the time for many of my fellow students.

By way of contrast, my perception as I left clinical practice in 2018 was that medicine had much more the feel of a business enterprise. The emphasis had changed. I can't point to a specific event that defines that transition. It began as a trickle with roots reaching back to the World War II era; in recent years it has seemed more like a river.

Unbeknownst to me and I'm sure to most people, the Supreme Court actually nudged this transition. Antitrust laws apply to business to prevent economic conspiracies. Competitive businesses are not supposed to improperly share information or engage in other activities that would allow them to reduce competition and take unfair advantage of consumers. It was in 1943 that the Court ruled that the American Medical

Association and the District of Columbia Medical Society violated antitrust law when they tried to limit a prepaid group practice that was developing in Washington. (See *A Second Opinion* – Arnold S. Relman, MD.)

This decision set the legal tone that was interpreted to support the notion that the profession of medicine could and should be treated as a business. The medical antitrust case was further supported thirty years later when there was a similar decision impacting the legal profession. The Court decided that the Virginia Bar Association was subject to antitrust regulation when it attempted to control some of the legal fees of its members.

In a way, these decisions were understandable because there are business aspects of any profession; however, the Court decisions were construed to apply not only to umbrella professional organizations, such as the American Medical Association or the American Bar Association, but also to individual physicians and attorneys, the associations' professional members.

That these legal precedents nourished the medical profession's move in a pro-business direction might not have been predicted by most of the 1940s and 1970s justices who participated in those decisions, but from small acorns big oak trees grow.

A second possible unintended consequence of these antitrust decisions was to "encourage" physicians to be very circumspect about speaking out against fellow physicians. If a physician is perceived as possibly incompetent or unethical, there has been a history of reluctance to professionally censure that physician because this could be litigated as interference with business freedoms, and therefore a violation of antitrust law. Fortunately, I believe that this reluctance to speak out, this particular lack of transparency, is on the wane.

I am deeply grateful to have had the opportunity to practice medicine. Despite my frustration about the business direction of medical practice, as I've said, the vast majority of my colleagues deserve a great deal of respect. Most physicians work hard and often shoulder heavy responsibility involving life and death. This is not easy.

Special interests cause the majority of price inflation, but physician behavior influences this as well. Physician-driven inflation was addressed in an insightful article written by Harvard surgeon, Atul Gawande. "The Cost Conundrum, What a Texas Town Can Teach Us About Health Care" was published in the June 1, 2009 issue of *The New Yorker* magazine. This tale of three cities compared Medicare costs per patient in the Texas towns of McAllen and El Paso (approximately 800 miles apart with similar demographics) and Grand Junction, Colorado.

In 2006, McAllen's Medicare cost per patient was almost $15,000; El Paso's was about half that amount (close to the national average at that time). To the north, Grand Junction's per capita cost was about $5,000, below the national average.

According to measurable parameters, which of these three communities produced the best care? Answer: Grand Junction at $5,000 per capita. Which produced the worst? Answer: McAllen Texas at $15,000 per capita. The difference in cost, it turns out, reflected the doctors' business attitudes and approach.

In high-cost McAllen, the physicians owned a number of the medical facilities that provided medical care, tests, and procedures. As usage of those facilities increased, so did the doctors' incomes. Were these entrepreneurial doctors ordering more services because of the financial benefit they reaped? Probably, even if only subconsciously.

According to Dr. Gawande, whatever their conscious or subconscious financial motives, these physicians felt they were providing good care and good value with their state-of-the-art medical centers. In fact, they had little idea how significantly per capita costs in McAllen exceeded those in the other towns.

I suspect that some, if not most, of McAllen physicians perceived no conflict of interest or compromise of integrity in their actions. Legally they probably had done nothing wrong. But they had been nourished educationally and professionally in a medical environment that subtly, or not so subtly, condoned a profit-driven model, an across-the-board approach to medical practice that predictably inflates the cost of medical care.

What about the more cost effective and higher quality care in Grand Junction? According to Gawande, physicians there approached their medical practice as professionals, with less emphasis on profit.

A few doctors in Grand Junction did advocate for a more business-oriented approach, but most of the Grand Junction group were willing to "leave money on the table" and choose more efficient delivery of quality care.

Gawande found that the variation in the cost of healthcare resulted from these differences of attitudes, values, professionalism, and perhaps even a degree of moral awareness on the part of the physicians. Dr. Gawande's intention clearly was not to criticize certain physicians, but to understand the problem in order to effect change.

Most physicians try to do what's right. Consider the story of Dr. Peter Eisenberg, my friend from college days who founded California Cancer Care, a large research-oriented oncology practice in Marin County. In 2006, Peter was recognized by *Forbes* magazine for taking an ethical stance that caused him a substantial loss of income; he rejected pharmaceutical giant Amgen's attempt to manipulate his medical prescribing ("Amgen's Enemies," *Forbes,* 10/30/06).

In 2008, he was invited to work with The Century Foundation on healthcare reform, a nonprofit, nonpartisan organization that sponsors and supervises timely analyses of economic policy, foreign affairs, and domestic political issues.

When Peter called to tell me about joining The Century Foundation to work on healthcare, he had no idea that I had begun writing about this topic. I remember well his prophetic words from that phone call: *If we're going to reform healthcare, all the big players, pharmaceuticals, insurance, hospitals, malpractice lawyers, and physicians will have to take a hit.* I agreed.

Around the same time, a young woman, then a senior in college, asked me for a letter of recommendation to medical school. I had known Jennifer for years and was happy to help. I requested a copy of her transcript and her application essays. Following is the first question on one application, and her written answer:

> **Question:** There are many problems facing healthcare in America today. Describe your interpretation of the status of healthcare in the United States today and those challenges the patients and the physicians of tomorrow will face.

Answer: A typical problem of healthcare in the United States today is that the healthcare system is run like a business with health insurance companies and HMOs seeking to maximize monetary gains as opposed to maximizing the quality of care for patients. Professionals with degrees in the field of business rather than physicians are making decisions regarding the rules and the administration of healthcare. Furthermore, primary care physicians are faced with the challenge of going through a myriad of healthcare provider agencies to obtain approval for necessary medical services for the patient.

Physicians of the future will face the challenge of taking control of decision-making and of administrating healthcare in our country. The power of making rules governing healthcare needs to be solely in the hands of physicians, who are the experts in healthcare – not businessmen, lobbyists, and politicians. In the interest of the quality of care for patients, the physicians need to make all decisions at every level regarding healthcare.

Primary Care Anemia

Obamacare made it possible for millions more patients to have insurance. If, as I hope, Obamacare finally gives way to Medicare, and eventually Medicare for All, America will have to absorb many more newly insured patients. This will further expose a major American problem: We have too few primary care physicians (PCPs) – pediatricians, family physicians, internists, and perhaps psychiatrists. Patients already have trouble seeing a primary care physician in a timely fashion. I believe that "physician extenders" (nurse practitioners and physician assistants) will appropriately relieve this shortfall to some degree, but patients will still seek expensive emergency treatment if their situation is urgent, or even not so urgent. Imagine what will happen with a new influx of patients.

After Romneycare (on which Obamacare was based) had been operating successfully for a number of years, there was an expectation that the number of emergency room visits in Massachusetts would be reduced as more patients became insured and began to see their own doctor.

The prediction was partly correct – as more patients became insured more medical care was sought. But relatively speaking, there were so few PCPs, patients either couldn't find a primary care physician, or couldn't find one who could see them promptly. So emergency room visits actually increased.

It is crucial that we expand the number of PCPs and add physician's assistants and nurse practitioners to the mix. These primary care professionals tend to care for patients in ways that promote health and prevent minor medical problems from developing into expensive medical emergencies. In this regard, we are currently worse off than many other nations.

A great disparity exists in the earnings of different medical specialties. Many physicians in no way fit the stereotype of the rich doctor. Overall, primary care physicians are at the lower end of the income totem pole. This has been especially responsible for the inadequate supply of PCPs.

Physician reimbursement is a touchy issue. Primary care physicians generally don't do expensive procedures. Their interaction with patients involves communicating and reflecting about that person's overall health picture. Ideally, they become the community's first line of healthcare defense, the first line of encouragement to promote wellness (preventive, protective health behaviors) and often the compassionate ears for community expressions of health concerns writ large. I call them our "thinking" doctors.

Most specialists do more procedures. I have called them "thinging" doctors. The "thingers" obviously do a lot of thinking but they bill patients mostly for interpreting imaging, performing surgery, or doing other types of procedures. Insurance reimbursement for "thinging" doctors is usually more than for "thinking" doctors.

My view over the last forty years, as the medical practice climate evolved, is that medical education has similarly evolved, becoming more accepting of this profit orientation. Current physicians often exit medical school in deep debt; that debt is an understandably powerful force. Medical students realize that PCPs are relatively as overworked as they are underpaid and that specialists make more money, sometimes a lot more money.

Earning potential, or lack thereof, is one reason many if not most medical students don't choose a career in primary care; they specialize instead, choosing "thinging" instead of "thinking."

A lead article in the Sunday, January 19, 2014 *The New York Times* told the story of a professor of history at the University of Central Arkansas who had a skin cancer removed. Her minor procedure required a few stitches, and somehow involved the services of three physicians – an ophthalmologist, a dermatologist, and an anesthesiologist, "thinging" doctors all.

The total bill exceeded $25,000. This is amazing and explains why some medical students these days speak of "the ROAD to success," ROAD being an acronym for radiology, ophthalmology, anesthesiology, and dermatology. They know where their financial bread is buttered.

These decisions made by medical students faced with hundreds of thousands of dollars of debt have profound public health/primary care implications. The potential for primary care physicians to improve their patients' quality of life and reduce overall health cost is significant and valuable. If there was to be a decrease of student debt and correction of the reimbursement inequity between PCPs and specialists, more medical students might choose to practice compassionate and gratifying primary care.

The recent announcement by NYU's medical school that students would no longer be required to pay tuition may start a positive trend in medical education. Also, largely led by Medicare and supported by Obamacare, the income disparity between primary care physicians and procedural physicians has been shrinking slowly.

Fee for Service vs. Salaried Medicine

American fee-for-service medicine is like piecework in factories. The subconscious mind has a powerful, even if largely invisible, influence on most lives, including physicians. When profit is acceptable and even a primary goal, as it is in United States healthcare, if that profit is based on the number of procedures you do, it is likely you will do more procedures; if profit depends on the number of patients you see in a day, it is likely you'll see more patients and therefore spend less time with each patient.

So, in America, with our profit-before-patients free market approach, and our fee-for-service urgency, what has happened? Time with patients creeps down, and the overall cost of medical care creeps up. This is not theory; this is our reality.

It is not realistic to believe that our fee-for-service, profit-before-patients model can be quickly transformed to the type of model employed by the Mayo Clinic, the Cleveland Clinic, or the Kaiser Permanente System in which physicians are salaried. In these respected institutions, the disparity of reimbursement between "thinking" and "thinging" is somewhat less. Perhaps with changing generations of medical students, new graduates may be leaning toward choosing salaried medical jobs in primary care or a specialty that allows more personal time for family.

Healthcare reform, expansion of Medicare, does not require that America give up its advantage in specialty care; it means that we can find ways to reward our primary care physicians more for the quality they bring to their practice and to their patients' lives.

A reorientation to medical professionalism is difficult as long as blindness about the failure of the free market in healthcare prevails. I believe physicians deserve to be well-compensated, but more because of hard work, skill, tremendous benefit to patients and professionalism, and less because of entrepreneurial attitudes.

Like Morris Fishbein in the 1949 *Meet the Press* interview, many physicians of the post-World War II era were probably evangelically pro-capitalism and anti-socialism. They would have needed a crystal ball to understand that the majority of American healthcare in 2021 is actually socialized. They would have been aghast and unconvinced that traditional capitalistic market-based healthcare just doesn't work well and contributes significantly to the unnecessary mediocrity of our American system. However, now we know.

The jury consists of twelve persons chosen to decide who has the better lawyer.

– Robert Frost

Chapter 9
Malpractice: The Doctor-Patient Cancer

Far too often the threat of malpractice invades the doctor-patient relationship, just as cancer invades healthy tissue. Simple awareness of the possibility of being sued has a chilling effect, breeding defensiveness, wariness, and mistrust, even if subconscious. This concern may not be part of every doctor-patient relationship, but it seems far more pervasive in American healthcare than I remember fifty years ago when I began medical practice.

I have a particular interest in legal matters. In the early years of my journey, the University of California allowed me to earn a law degree at Berkeley while concurrently completing my psychiatry training at the medical school in San Francisco. I began teaching forensic psychiatry in the Bay Area. I soon realized, however, that despite my fascination with medical-legal issues, I enjoyed seeing patients much more.

Except for rare forays into legal areas, especially in my writing, my work returned almost exclusively to clinical medicine, first in San Francisco, then in Vermont during the 1980s, and now in Florida. Over these many years, however, I've thought a great deal about how we might cure the malpractice cancer.

The nonfinancial consequences of our litigious environment – the doctor's fear, silence, and guilt along with the patient's doubt and mistrust – are not fully appreciated by the public and possibly by many physicians, even as they and their patients are victimized.

Despite the billions of dollars of higher healthcare costs because of defensive medicine, the real culprit in this cancerous environment has been the slow, inexorable deterioration of the doctor-patient relationship.

The essence of a healthy doctor-patient relationship is respectful, cordial, compassionate, honest, and reciprocal communication. Ideally, mutual understanding and trust develop between the patient seeking treatment and the doctor seeking to provide it.

The importance of this human connection cannot be overemphasized. Over the course of the years I've spent in healthcare, however, I have witnessed the subtle, or not so subtle, decline of the qualities that promote trust and basic respect between doctor and patient. I believe the seminal force undermining the doctor-patient relationship can be directly traced to the growth of the malpractice industry. Also feeding the cancer is the previously noted relationship of the malpractice environment to our hurried money-driven, profit-first healthcare environment that contributes to a lessening of listening by the doctor, resulting in patient skepticism and annoyance.

Doctors will never be able to practice medicine flawlessly; consistently impeccable technique, perfect comprehension, and imperturbable attentiveness are simply beyond human potential. We should, however, identify the tiny minority of physicians who fail repeatedly, and have these physicians seek further education or leave the patient-related practice of medicine. This problematic minority should be distinguished from the majority of doctors whose rare failures result from a lack of perfection because we're all imperfect humans.

Many excellent doctors become upset and guilt-ridden by the thought that they might have injured someone or done less than their best work; but all too often doctors are afraid to express their feelings or to express any regret because they fear the malpractice exposure.

Defensive Medicine

Our malpractice cancer causes extra medical expenses to add up. Physicians order more tests and consultations without which, if they missed anything, they could be more legally vulnerable. A few years ago, when I began to write my recent series of books about problems with our healthcare system, I spoke at length about this with a neurologist. He told me that his hospital work had become increasingly demanding because so many hospital specialists, called "hospitalists," refer hospitalized patients to him about almost anything neurological. They practice defensive medicine, consulting the neurologist (and presumably other specialists) immediately, even when the hospitalists themselves are quite capable of recognizing and initially managing many of the problems.

I asked the neurologist, "In your opinion what percentage of your hospital consults are medically unnecessary or premature?"

"Maybe as much as 40 percent," he said.

It's a surprising figure. Unnecessary consultations cost as much as appropriate ones. Therefore, this sort of consultation pattern inflates costs and doesn't necessarily produce better outcomes.

Both "thinging and thinking" doctors practice defensive medicine. Specialists (the "thingers") practice differently than PCPs (the "thinkers"), partly because venturing beyond their specialty's narrow boundaries may invite malpractice lawsuits should anything go wrong.

Conversely, some primary care office physicians, like hospitalists, tend not to treat problems they could treat very well. Defensive medicine dictates that to minimize malpractice risk, treatment of even some less complicated problems best be referred to a specialist. A poor treatment outcome achieved by any PCP exposes those doctors not only to scrutiny of their medical skills, but also to inquiry about the soundness of their judgment if something goes wrong, and they chose *not* to consult a specialist.

These referrals can be costly, and as in the example of the neurologist, not always medically necessary. But extra cost and deterioration of the doctor-patient relationship represent only two aspects of the malpractice problem. This cancer has a third impact, an insidious influence on how doctors think about medical care, and how we practice.

The best medical decisions require knowledge, first and foremost, but not all treatment can or should be exactly by the book. Because patients are infinitely variable, medical decisions often require creative, customized, thoughtful, and occasionally courageous solutions.

Historically, clinical improvements come from thinking creatively about individual patients in real time, developing new ideas, then testing these ideas using sound research principles. The term *evidence-based medicine* refers to principles that have been confirmed scientifically. Evidence-based medicine is the core of careful clinical practice. It is necessary and worthwhile, but it is not perfect. Occasionally the evidence turns out to be incorrect. Yet I know physicians who explicitly state that they will never do anything outside the box (meaning they will not act as creatively as they might) because they could be sued more easily if anything went wrong. As a result, patients are sometimes denied the benefit of professional, medically creative thinking that recognizes their individuality.

Sadly, when creative thought becomes too risky, for some physicians everything in the current medical playbook becomes sacrosanct. It's easy to begin to practice more automatically. Dogmatism and fear explain how medical practice sometimes gets dumbed down and accused of being rote, impersonal, and reflexive. Certainly not all physicians have this attitude, but any diminished sensitivity to the idiosyncrasy of each patient as a unique person is unfortunate.

Our doctor-patient cancer is not being effectively treated. It continues to grow, and there is no surgery, no chemotherapy, no radiation, no targeted biologic missile, no genetic reordering, no herbal suppression, and no spontaneous immunologic miracle anywhere in the Affordable Care Act or elsewhere that will soon lift the malpractice cloud.

The family of a wonderful physician who I knew of in my younger days told me his story, but preferred that he remains anonymous. A few years ago, when this prominent retired elderly physician encountered some relatively minor but significant (for his age) medical problems, he was admitted to the same prestigious teaching hospital to which he had dedicated many years of his life. He had been one of the most distinguished professors at the medical school, but most of the physicians at this university, now twenty years past his retirement, did not know him.

Up to that hospitalization, he had been active

and mentally sharp, playing golf every day, learning Spanish, reading, and playing bridge. Although he was nearly ninety years of age, he seemed much younger.

During the early part of that hospitalization, he felt the care he received was spotty and disengaged. Over the fifty years of his medical career, this doctor had built a reputation as a brilliant diagnostician. However, when he made some outside-the-box suggestions as to the specifics of his care, he was rebuffed by his young attending physician.

As the days passed, he became weaker and all the more frustrated at being ignored. He soon became depressed and convinced that medicine, which had been a calling for him, had largely become no more than a "lucrative business."

One night he rang for a nurse who did not come. Finally, he got out of bed to go to the bathroom and slipped, falling and breaking a hip. Without surgery he would never walk adequately again.

This was unacceptable. He wanted to live, walk well, and continue his fine quality of life, and if that result required more extensive surgery, he wanted it. He fully understood his choices and was willing to take the chance of dying on the operating table in order to recover as fully as possible. He made that known.

The best chance to preserve his physical prowess would have been a total hip replacement. But the prevailing surgical wisdom for a man his age was to opt for a shorter but predictably less effective surgery; this was a safe decision, perhaps difficult to criticize, but not tailored to this particular individual.

His surgeon insisted on the conservative approach, a repair but not the total replacement. The elderly doctor reluctantly agreed. The surgery went well – so well in fact it seemed likely that he would have easily tolerated the longer surgery required for a total hip replacement. After the surgeon broke two orthopedic saws during the procedure, he commented that the ninety-year-old had "bones of steel."

As it turned out the surgery was "successful," but the doctor never again walked well. Life as he had known it ended. He deteriorated rapidly, unhappily, and died six months after that surgery.

We will never know if this physician's clinical suggestions about his own medical care would have changed the outcome of his illness and recovery. We will never know if his life would have been different had he received the hip replacement he wanted. We will never know for sure if he would have actually lived longer. But it is clear that his surgeon was more comfortable with the legally conservative approach, the in-the-box approach, rather than with the more extensive hip replacement desired by this very sophisticated patient and his family.

The "safe" decision is easy and almost automatic these days, especially when a physician has been nudged and nurtured for so many years by our litigious environment. As a consequence, the individual, more creative approach for the more unusual patient may lose out.

Malpractice Insurance for All

Malpractice awards by juries can be unpredictably high, exceeding the limits of malpractice insurance. Physicians' life savings can be wiped out. Private malpractice insurance doesn't always protect physicians from catastrophic financial loss. The fear is palpable. That's why doctors are afraid and become so defensive;

that's why this cancer grows.

Tort law deals with personal injury, including medical malpractice. Over the years, any suggestion to reduce malpractice liability by changing tort law or putting a cap on the amount of money that could be awarded by a jury has been strenuously resisted by one special interest group: malpractice plaintiffs' attorneys. The plaintiffs' bar will go to hell and back, and to the bank and back, to resist malpractice reform. If I were to ask myself who benefits most from the malpractice environment in the United States, the answer remains clear, and was always the same: attorneys.

Doctors are not the only casualties of the malpractice war. I believe it is appropriate that patients who suffer from consequential malpractice should be supported and compensated. All too often, however, attorneys won't represent an injured patient whose case does not appear likely to lead to either a predictable legal victory, a large financial judgment, or both.

A few years ago, as my appreciation of Medicare blossomed, a peculiar idea began to take shape, and I asked myself a clarifying question: does our malpractice environment benefit our healthcare system in any way?

At the Chautauqua Institute in 2013, I listened to Dr. Harvey Fineberg, then president of the Institute of Medicine. He reported no evidence that the threat or accomplishment of malpractice litigation had in any way contributed to improvement of the practice of medicine; defensive medicine only distorted practice and raised overall costs.

The next question I asked myself was a doozy: If Medicare were implemented, might the government appropriately cover malpractice expense and liability for all physicians? Medicare would be the primary-payer insurance for the United States. All (or almost all) physicians would be working under the umbrella of government; might that justify consideration of automatic government-supported malpractice protection? What may seem at first like a wild idea, maybe too compassionate to physicians, isn't actually a big stretch and may benefit most patients a great deal.

Under state umbrellas, governments already pay for

the malpractice coverage of thousands of physicians working in universities and elsewhere. Under federal umbrellas, thousands of physicians serving in the Veterans Administration, the Army, Navy, Air Force, Marines, the U.S. Public Health Service, and the National Institutes of Health are fully covered. Why wouldn't expansion of this government malpractice protection to Medicare participating physicians be possible?

Doctors might be pleased with this plan. If doctors' incomes are constrained under Medicare, having no malpractice premiums would be welcome. As noted, most doctors work hard, often bearing a life-and-death responsibility that few other professionals experience. Also, as suggested, most physicians do not make serious mistakes often, if ever. However, that tiny minority I spoke about make substantially more mistakes than others. With the government as insurer, those physicians with repeated poor performance would be identified far more quickly and transparently. Red flags would pop up.

If human nature holds true, protecting doctors from fear of possible financial devastation would reduce defensive medical spending. But even if malpractice reform measures were instituted today, change in the behavior of physicians would take substantial time. It probably would require new generations of doctors, who didn't begin their practice under the malpractice cloud, for defensive medical practice to recede and the doctor-patient relationship to improve.

The calculus of a law firm in deciding not to pursue a malpractice action if they don't envision a predictable victory (or the case is not worth enough money to justify the law firm's expense in prosecuting) is not always fair. If this malpractice coverage idea was pursued, although statutory tort law itself wouldn't necessarily change, it is generally accepted that suing the government is difficult. This may make it even less attractive for attorneys to pursue cases, and therefore more difficult for some patients to receive financial compensation through litigation. But this is a double-edged sword.

In recent years, interest is growing in the developing legal field of arbitration and alternative dispute resolution. Some practices already ask patients to sign arbitration agreements. Depending upon what new Medicare rules are eventually adopted, patients could realistically present their grievances to a law firm or a professional arbitration board for an analysis, *or both.* Patients could then decide whether or not to pursue litigation, mediation, arbitration, or drop the case. Thus, having alternatives to litigation and giving patients opportunity to seek recovery beyond the financially-driven "wisdom" of a law firm could offer patients more options, a better view of their situation, and an improved opportunity for appropriate help.

For our economy, the potential reduction of medical cost if defensive medical practices were reduced could be substantial. According to PNHP (Physicians for a National Health Program), these annual costs are estimated at $46 billion, far less than I had heard previously.

My own unscientific inflated estimate of the amount added to per capita healthcare cost was about 10 percent; other physicians guessed as high as 37 percent. Maybe these inflated estimates reflect a larger subconscious impact on our thinking, an outsized fear that we're missing something, and a reluctance to engage creative individualistic thought that might be more "dangerous." Perhaps this less creative attitude, this intrusion into the doctor-patient relationship, and our hidden subconscious concerns represent the totality cost of our malpractice malignancy. Still, even $46 billion is not pocket change, and the cost of the communication cancer is incalculable.

Practically speaking, the annual cost of malpractice awards in the U.S. is estimated to be about $10 billion. For the government to pick up the $10 billion malpractice tab, and save part of the $46 billion, seems like a good deal; the cost of providing malpractice protection for all doctors serving the government would be substantially less than the dollar savings attributable to the reduction of defensive medical practice.

I have no illusions. I fully appreciate that the transformation of the United States healthcare to a Medicare primary-payer system, in and of itself will be daunting – truly a road less traveled. I also understand that the malpractice insurance protections I have suggested to help heal the doctor-patient cancer and reduce billions of dollars of defensive medical costs might be viewed by some as naive or unrealistic.

As I've lived with this idea over the past few years, however, I've gone from "this is such a long shot" to "this might eventually be doable." Both patients and physicians could benefit emotionally and financially. Finally, we just might cure the malpractice cancer.

A hospital bed is a parked taxi with the meter running.

– Groucho Marx

Chapter 10
Hospitals

Before Senator Obama became a candidate for president, he expressed a preference for Medicare for All. At some point during his presidential evolution, he realized that would have been politically impossible.

The passage of the Affordable Care Act was made possible only by political compromise. In order to reduce opposition from special interest groups, deals were made (especially with the insurance industry) that allowed medically-related corporations to maintain good profit margins.

These deals yielded two main results: first, the legislation passed; second, Obamacare remained wedded to the free market delusion that we could fix our problems by continuing to allow healthcare to be run for the benefit of corporations, instead of what's best for patients and the economy.

I am going to share a half dozen hospital-related stories that reflect this uniquely American situation. The stories all represent the hospital as a main character playing on the stage with other special interests, most consistently insurance companies. Some of you, like me, will be upset when you read these hospital-related tales. I wish I could tell you that these stories represent egregious, excessive, or rare situations, that they are not fair portrayals of our system. Unfortunately, I do not believe that's the case.

Story One: Liver Transplant

In 2012, Marty Makary, MD, a Harvard-Georgetown trained surgeon, now at Johns Hopkins wrote *Unaccountable: What Hospitals Won't Tell You and*

How Transparency Can Revolutionize Healthcare. Dr. Makary's disclosures emphasize lack of transparency related to quality of hospital services. Even as a physician, I found his disclosures about behind-the-scenes dysfunction of hospitals and some physicians disquieting:

> "Back in 2002, Mount Sinai Hospital...was considered by many in surgery to be the best liver-donor transplant center in America, a judgment that might have even been true – in the daytime. But at night it was a different story. Chasing profits like so many other hospitals, Mount Sinai chose to shrink nurse ratios from one nurse for every six patients to one nurse for every seven. And its unsafe overnight operation relied on only one intern. (In the hospital where I trained, the staff all knew the first-year surgery intern working the night shift on the transplant service was overworked and spread way too thin.)
>
> Tragedy arrived one night when the intern on call for transplant surgery, just months out of medical school, was in charge of covering thirty-

four complex patients. The overwhelmed intern didn't know how to handle it. For hours she failed to call her senior surgeons to ask for advice. Tragically, Michael Hurewitz (age 57), who had donated part of his healthy liver to his brother, wound up choking on the blood he was vomiting, and died.

In many hospitals, interns are discouraged from asking senior physicians for help even when they desperately need it. Hurewitz's preventable death was a tragedy resulting from a poor teamwork culture, a system of poorly backed doctors and nurses spread too thin, and a management that had no good mechanism to elicit staff-safety concerns.

A state investigation uncovered ninety-two complaints about Mount Sinai Hospital: seventy-five were about the liver-transplant unit and sixty-two of them involved patient deaths...as Georgetown residents we were not surprised at all. On the contrary, we were members of similar setups for disaster and knew what happened at Mount Sinai could have happened at many reputable hospitals.

> There are bad doctors and impaired doctors, but the problem of doctors making repeated avoidable mistakes is a hospital management problem. Not only do unsafe hospital systems allow bad and impaired doctors to keep on practicing, they foster situations in which even good doctors will make mistakes."

This episode that Dr. Makary reported a number of years ago is emblematic of the nontransparent complexity that in some instances reflects that profit first patients second approach that too often drives healthcare decisions.

Mount Sinai's transplant unit had a fine reputation, and the Hurewitz brothers may have appropriately relied on that to some degree. But let's suppose that they were remarkably sophisticated consumers, far more sophisticated than most of us, and did additional due diligence. What might they have asked before the surgery? The following questions are intended to demonstrate why buying healthcare is far more intricate than buying other goods and services:

- Did Mr. Hurewitz know the number of similar operations his surgeon had done, and how that compared to other local surgeons, or surgeons elsewhere?

- Did he know the complication rate his surgeon's patients experienced?

- Did he know whether resident physicians would participate in the surgery, and if so, what their level of training was, and what their participation would be?

- Did he know that Mount Sinai had seventy-five complaints about their transplant unit, sixty-two of which involved deaths?

- Did he know that his emergency care would be handled by a member of the transplant service, who might be an intern, rather than by one of the emergency physicians at the hospital?

- Did he know the infection rate of the surgical

suites at Mount Sinai?

- Did he know how the overall infection rate in Mount Sinai compared to other hospitals?

It is perhaps unlikely that many patients could or would launch the sort of investigation I'm suggesting. But every question is relevant. Answers are available, but often difficult to obtain.

That last issue, the question of hospital infection is important but rarely gets public attention. Hospitals that do have higher infection rates in general, or specifically in their operating suites, don't want the public to know. In Wyoming in 2011, one hospital was found to have performed hundreds of surgeries for which standard sterilization procedures were not followed in the operating suite.

When this was discovered, the hospital simply corrected its sterile technique. Then a whistleblower came forward, starting a chain of events that eventually led the Center for Disease Control (CDC) in Atlanta to require the hospital to notify all exposed patients, and offer free screening for HIV and Hepatitis B and

C. The hospital's initial inaction – to avoid exposure to malpractice liability, limit damage to its reputation and, consequently to its bottom line – is a clear reflection of its priority: profit was more important than patients.

Any improvement in healthcare transparency will be a blessing in terms of informed decision-making. However, there are two previously mentioned nagging obstructions to achieving the kind of transparency in healthcare compared to other economic sectors: first, the enormous complexity of healthcare; second, the frequent pressures of medical urgency or emergency that don't allow time for due diligence.

Story Two: Outpatient Hospital Profits

A friend said to me, "I've had some symptoms that could be heart-related and my cardiologist ordered tests and referred me to his hospital's imaging center. I asked the price and was told the charge would be $4,000. I was shocked. My insurance would pay most of it, but I'd be left with a substantial bill. Got any suggestions?"

I advised him to call the director at an independent imaging center who I knew well and ask how much his center charges for the same exams. I had a hunch the cost would be less, and I knew that the independent imaging center was first class, with equipment that was then newer and of higher quality than that at the hospital. When my friend called me back, he said, "I couldn't believe it. I was quoted $500 for exactly the same exam."

The friend who asked me that question is a veterinarian, a sophisticated consumer, and he knew the right questions to ask about imaging. I was able to help him with cost and quality assessment. But most patients have a completely different experience.

Had he not asked me for a suggestion, the referral of the cardiologist to an expensive imaging center owned by the hospital that employed him would likely have been accepted. This is quite routine, though I'm not at all sure the referring physician actually knew that his hospital's imaging was so much more expensive, and perhaps of lesser quality. Lack of access to healthcare price and quality information is the rule, not the exception among patients and often among doctors.

In the wake of my friend's experience, I asked a colleague (whose practice had been purchased by a local hospital) whether he was required contractually to refer patients to physicians and testing facilities within that hospital system. "No," he said, "there's nothing in our contract specifically requiring that. When you work in a system it is only natural to refer within that system, but I have never been asked." He suddenly paused. "Actually," he continued, "an administrator noticed that I had referred some patients to physical therapy services outside the hospital, and he asked me to consider using the hospital's service."

"I explained that some patients had complained that hospital physical therapy was too expensive, and they preferred to use less expensive outside physical therapy services they had used before. I asked the administrator if his facility could lower its prices to competitive levels. He was reluctant to promise anything, saying only that he would work with patients whose insurance was inadequate or who had real hardship."

The *TIME* Stories

On March 4, 2013, *TIME* magazine published what was purportedly their lengthiest article ever, "Bitter Pill: Why Medical Bills Are Killing Us" by Steven Brill. After reading the complete article, I felt even more confirmed that a functional free market in American healthcare is a myth. (See also Mr. Brill's book: *America's Bitter Pill: Money, Politics, Backroom Deals, and the Fight to Fix Our Broken Healthcare.)*

When we receive a hospital bill we're often astounded by the figure. The first impulse is to ask how we are going to pay it. Mr. Brill explored the central question that lurks behind the charges: Why are our hospital bills (or most medical bills in America) so high in the first place?

We all understand that hospitals charge a lot of money. What may at first seem surprising is that hospitals, on average, only collect about 35 to 55 percent of the amount they charge. Most of that 35 percent comes from insurance companies that always want to pay less for inpatient care, but also want to inflate premiums. There is a tendency for hospitals to charge higher fees to those who do pay to make up any shortfall. However, Mr. Brill makes it very clear that the thirty-five percent the hospital does collect is still big money – very big money.

Hospital up-charging is also encouraged by large capital expenses such as major building programs (sometimes conceived to outdo the next guy) and huge payrolls. But until this article in *TIME* penetrated the veil of secrecy, the familiar lack of transparency made it difficult to determine whether those expenses justify the prices we are charged.

Hospitals are required by law, and usually by the consciences of their healthcare professionals, to provide health services to patients who have no insurance or means to pay. This pro bono service is founded in admirable and humane practice, but sometimes hospitals justify a lot of their high prices by claiming that their pro bono work results in a financial shortfall, from which they must recover. So, as noted above, those of us who can pay are charged more to cover the costs that come from treating those who have no insurance, or inadequate insurance. We are charged outrageous rates for an aspirin tablet, a bag of intravenous solution, the use of an operating room, and many of its outpatient services.

Do hospitals deserve to make these substantial upcharges to cover their charitable efforts? I'll acknowledge that such a question is very complex, but I'll ask you to come to your own inclination based on the following information provided by Mr. Brill.

Pro bono work is provided to patients who can't pay, does cost hospitals money. However, per the *TIME* article, the hospitals inflate these contributions by calculating the dollars they "contribute" based on their high retail charge for every service, as opposed to the hospital's actual bare bones cost to provide this pro bono work.

According to the *TIME* article, on average the actual cost to hospitals of those "free" services they blame for inflated prices across the board is about half a percent of the hospital's total income. *TIME* reported that the millions of charitable dollars many hospitals receive each year amount to about one percent of their total income. This would mean that many hospitals receive more in charitable contributions than the dollars actually required to provide the charitable care.

In addition to the hospitals' charitable contributions, the federal government had been helping hospitals with substantial subsidies to ease the burden of their unpaid care. Hospitals are often allowed to charge much more than independent nonhospital facilities for similar services based on their charitable costs; perhaps this needs review. (Remember my veterinarian friend.)

With Obamacare, some of the subsidies previously provided to hospitals to cover pro bono and lower-paid work were eliminated. The expansion of Medicaid under the Affordable Care Act (which many state governors refused to implement) was intended to increase the number of paying customers, adding even more money to hospital coffers.

The expansion of Medicaid would have more than made up for the reduction of government subsidies. However, in those states where governors refused to accept Medicaid dollars available through Obamacare, not only are many patients left out in the cold, their hospitals are twice-cursed – they get neither the money intended to come from more Medicaid patients, nor the subsidies they previously received from the government. (Talk about cutting off your nose to spite your face.)

TIME author Steven Brill became curious about hospital costs and healthcare costs in general during a visit to Houston in 2012. He noticed skyscrapers and learned that these towers were but a few of the 240 buildings on the 1,300-acre Texas Health Science campus, a part of the vast University of Texas Education System. The famous "nonprofit" MD Anderson Cancer Center is located on that campus.

When the article was written about seven years ago, the president of MD Anderson earned a salary of $1.84 million. The CEO of the entire University of Texas system earned $674,350 at that time. (I suspect the Texas football coach made more than both combined.)

The *TIME* article is the source of the final four hospital stories; many more stories are in the original article. As you read about these four patients, please note that only one patient was uninsured; the other three were "insured." Two of the three patients who were insured and the one uninsured patient faced financial devastation. Only one insured patient, the one with Medicare, was well-covered.

Story Three: Sean (Insured)

In 2012, Sean was diagnosed with non-Hodgkins lymphoma at age forty-two. He and his wife had started their own business shortly before his diagnosis. The only insurance they could afford was the type of private insurance that provides an illusion that you are adequately covered and didn't meet the higher standards of the Affordable Care Act. (It was policies such as these that were prohibited soon after the implementation of Obamacare.)

MD Anderson, the nonprofit flagship of the University of Texas Health Science campus, wouldn't accept Sean's insurance. They required payment in advance of $83,900 for a treatment plan and initial chemotherapy. The $83,900 charge included $15,000 for blood and other laboratory testing, for which Medicare would have paid only a few hundred dollars. Sean was too young for Medicare coverage, but those few hundred dollars would have covered, nearly or completely, the actual cost to the hospital of performing those tests.

Back when records were kept on paper, that

$15,000 charge would have been specified in MD Anderson's mammoth *chargemaster* book that listed every possible charge in that hospital. Now chargemasters are computerized. Every hospital bill is calculated using prices in this internal charge list, and every chargemaster is unique to its hospital. The chargemasters share one common and consistent characteristic: they all generate prices far in excess of the actual cost of any product or service.

Even though the hospital may collect only a portion of their total inflated charges, per the *TIME* article, that portion is usually sufficient to insure the hospital remains profitable. It's a windfall for the hospital, a financial catastrophe for some patients, and fuel to the fire of healthcare cost inflation. Obamacare does not change this; Medicare does.

Medicare does not change the "chargemasters run wild" problem, but often because of more government transparency about real costs, and because Medicare is designed (when not legislatively prevented) to protect patients and the economy, Medicare reduces the allowed payment, usually providing a little more than the actual cost for the service provided. This reduces the amount that the government approves and pays, thus reducing significantly the amount patients have to pay out of pocket. Medicare is actually fairer to patients and our economy than the Affordable Care Act or our Assholistic pre-Obamacare nonsystem.

Sean and his wife Stephanie were fortunate in that they were able to borrow the $83,900 from family.

Story Four: Janet S. (Uninsured)

Janet was evaluated for chest pain in the Stamford Connecticut Hospital emergency department. At age sixty-four, she was one year shy of Medicare eligibility. Janet spent a total of three hours in the hospital. The good news – her diagnosis was indigestion. The bad news – almost $21,000 in bills divided as follows: $995 for the ambulance, $3,000 for the physicians, and $17,000 for the hospital.

As a former emergency physician, I understand that evaluation of a possible heart attack requires a series of lab tests. In Janet's case, a specific enzyme was tested. It rises rapidly and remains elevated for a few hours during and just after a heart attack. This test was performed three times while Janet was in the ER, and fortunately the initial level was normal and did not rise.

Stamford's chargemaster set the price of each enzyme test to be $199.50, so the three tests represented $598.50 of the $17,000 total hospital charges. Had Janet been a year older, Medicare would have paid the hospital $13.94 for each test, grand total of $41.18.

According to Mr. Brill, hospital administrators grouse about Medicare's (congressionally supervised) underpayments, but according to the Department of Health and Human Services, Medicare rates, while not maximizing hospital profit margin, do cover actual hospital costs.

Stamford Hospital reported in 2010 that its total charges for lab work were $293.2 million. The total cost to the hospital of providing those tests was reported as $27.5 million.

Unfortunately, Janet was unemployed and uninsured at the time of this hospital visit. Had she been insured under a policy that paid some of the charges, her total payment due would have been less than $21,000 to begin with because insurance companies negotiate discounts. The discounts they receive do not begin to approach the real (lower) costs reflected by Medicare payments, but they do provide some help for the insured. Thus, ironically and almost cruelly, patients like Janet and Sean, who are uninsured or underinsured, are sometimes asked to pay the whole bill, while those of us with quality insurance policies or Medicare have built-in discounts and pay much less out of pocket.

Story Five: Steve H. (Insured)

Steve was a retail store worker in his thirties when Mr. Brill wrote about him. His back pain led him to undergo an outpatient procedure to implant a pain control device at Mercy Hospital in Oklahoma City. In 2011, Steve's insurance had an annual payout limit (cap) of $60,000. Steve had over $45,000 of coverage remaining for the year and assumed the procedure could cost no more than $10,000. He was wrong and didn't ask.

His insurance paid $3 for a (presumably) reusable marking pen used to indicate the incision site, $32 for a (presumably) reusable blanket to keep him warm during the procedure, $31 for a (presumably) reusable strap to secure Steve on the table during the procedure, and $39 for the gown the surgeon wore (available online for $6). Steve's bill also included a $6,289 facility fee that should have included most or all of these individually billed items. Essentially, he seemed to be double-billed.

The *TIME* article documents many more remarkable detailed charges. The real whopper was the $49,237 paid for the implantable neurostimulator, which afforded the hospital a medical device profit of about $30,000. Steve's total hospital bill, excluding doctors' fees, was $86,951, which exceeded his policy cap and left him personally financially liable for about $40,000.

One of the key benefits of Obamacare is that it prohibits caps, those annual or lifetime payout limits in insurance policies. (Medicare does not have such caps.) Unfortunately, in 2011 and before implementation of Obamacare, Steve's insurance company was able to put that $60,000 annual cap on the amount they would pay out. Keep in mind, as with most of the other patients discussed so far, Steve was insured. Is it any wonder that the majority of personal bankruptcy filings in the United States are related to medical bills?

While Obamacare does eliminate caps on the amount a policy will pay, it does not completely eliminate all high deductible insurance policies with substantial copays. When you add together high deductibles and high copays, because they are a percentage of astronomical prices, medically-related bankruptcy still occurs. Because of lower deductibles and copays based on the lower amounts that Medicare pays with no caps, our current Medicare system does not lead to medically-related bankruptcy.

Story Six: Alan A. (Medicare Insured)

At age seventy-eight, Alan was diagnosed with non-Hodgkins lymphoma (like patient Sean). At the time of the article, Alan was eighty-eight – a cancer survivor who required ongoing treatment.

Every six weeks, Alan traveled to Memorial Sloan Kettering Cancer Center in New York City to receive Flebogamma, a drug that kept him alive for a decade.

His charge was $4,615 for the Flebogamma each visit, plus a $340 doctor charge at every other visit.

The procedure takes five hours, and he was charged $414 per hour for a nurse to administer the medicine. There were always two other patients, sometimes three, who were cared for by that same nurse at the same time, and they also paid $414 per hour for their nursing care. In other words that nurse was generating more than $1,600 per hour for the hospital.

Sloan Kettering acknowledged that the nursing charges were "complex" and meant in part to cover the "discounts" for Medicare and Medicaid patients who represent about a third of their patients. So every six weeks, the chargemaster billed Alan about $7,346 for the drugs, the doctors' fees, nursing fees, and other items.

I'm going to simplify a complex calculation. Of the $7,346 Sloan Kettering charged Alan, Medicare reduced the liability to a total of $2,425. Of that amount Medicare paid $1,938, Alan's private supplemental policy paid $438.50, and Alan paid $48.50 out of pocket.

The cost of the Flebogamma probably represented

a substantial portion of the $2,425 that Medicare found allowable. By law for Medicare patients, the government must pay the hospital the "average sales price" for the medication nationally, plus a 6 percent bonus. The average sales price of a drug is determined by a very complicated calculation, and much of the data for that calculation was provided by the drug company. Assuming that drug price is quite inflated as is the rule rather than the exception, this represents an example, even with Medicare, of how the government is forced to buy into an inflated healthcare market – another pharmaceutical lobbying victory.

But there's more to Alan's story. Unfortunately, Alan also suffered a heart attack and was hospitalized at Virtua Marlton Hospital near my hometown, Philadelphia. This is a for-profit hospital, part of a group of four hospitals that in 2010 generated $633.7 million in revenue, yielding an operating profit of $91 million. The CEO was paid $3,073,000.

Chargemaster calculated Alan's total heart attack bill to be $268,227. Medicare reviewed the bill and paid Virtua Marlton $43,320. Alan paid a total of $100 to the hospital for incidental expenses. If we all had Medicare, we could save a ton of money. I know that seems counterintuitive because we hear constantly that Medicare is running out of money but, as you will learn, that view is very shortsighted.

About twenty-five years ago, I attended a lecture given by the CEO of a very large hospital system in Jacksonville. I listened with rapt attention as he explained that private hospital costs went up as a result of Medicare having reduced payments. I'm sure that is true, but I didn't know then what I know now. The hospitals may have raised prices not necessarily because they were motivated to cover costs, but perhaps even more likely to maintain their profit margins (see Chapter 14).

In the Case of Alan A. who was covered by Medicare, Mr. Brill reports that despite Medicare's reduced payments, Sloan Kettering still made something like a 50 percent profit. So, even though Medicare saves money by paying less, it presumably is paying its way, but not as much as special interests like hospitals, drug companies, or equipment manufacturers are used to.

As Steven Brill points out, a core problem in

American healthcare is that our prices are too high. I completely agree. As discussed, all medical charges in America will continue to rise because the healthcare free market has those oversized gas pedals but only tiny brakes. Price gouging is easy when the free market doesn't work.

The pharmaceutical industry likes to depict itself as a research-based industry, as the source of innovative drugs. Nothing could be further from the truth. This is their incredible PR and their nerve.

– Marcia Angell

Chapter 11
Drug Problems

The words "special interests" as related to healthcare identifies businesses like hospitals, health insurance companies and pharmaceutical corporations that have special interest in making the most healthcare profit possible. In speaking of drug problems, I am not referring to the current opioid epidemic, but one of the more massive special interests in healthcare, the pharmaceutical industry.

In June 2006, the *New England Journal of Medicine*

published a comment authored by the late Democratic Congresswoman Louise Slaughter, who held a master's degree in public health. Congresswoman Slaughter shone a light on the kind of political process that contributes significantly to our financially bloated and dysfunctional healthcare delivery system.

According to Ms. Slaughter, the House Commerce Committee refused to consider fifty-eight of the fifty-nine amendments put forward by both Republicans and Democrats to strengthen the bill that finally provided coverage for some of the cost of medication for Medicare recipients (Medicare Part D). She wrote: "Among those rejected amendments was one requiring Medicare to use beneficiaries' collective purchasing power to negotiate lower (medication) prices, and another amendment which would have allowed Americans to import less expensive prescription medication from Canada."

Other allegations included allowing representatives of Big Pharma (the Pharmaceutical Research and Manufacturers of America or PhRMA) into the meetings of the Committee on Energy and Commerce from which some Democratic congressmen were excluded, sometimes even "physically barred from the deliberations."

According to Congressman Slaughter, while this was happening, the Committee's chairman decided to leave Congress and negotiated a deal for a $2 million a year job as a lobbyist with PhRMA, and a Commerce Committee aide who helped author the Medicare Part D legislation also left his position, once the legislation was passed, to also work for PhRMA as a lobbyist.

Finally, she reported that the chief actuary of CMS (Centers for Medicare and Medicaid Services) deflated estimates of expected costs for the program by $134 billion because of an alleged threat he would lose his job if he gave Congress the real figures.

Before Medicare Part D, physicians witnessed situations in which older patients were hospitalized because they could not afford to take the medications they needed. Although Medicare Part D has definitely helped, during the so-called "donut hole" when the patient has to resume paying for their medication until they spend a certain amount of additional money, some multi-medicated seniors still abandon or reduce needed medication because of prescription costs.

When finally passed, the 2006 Medicare Part D legislation *precluded* price negotiation with pharmaceutical corporations. Thus, when our government purchases the same medications for Medicare patients or Veterans Administration patients, the medications for the VA cost a lot less.

This is just a single example of the power of a special interest, in this case pharmaceutical corporations, to control and distort legislation that removes Hippocratic consideration from the process. The result is neither patient friendly nor fiscally fair to taxpayers; it is a bitter pill we shouldn't have to swallow.

PhRMA's usual justification for high profit is the claim that profits are funneled into much-needed research and development (R&D). There is a basis for this argument, but it's not as straightforward as it appears. PhRMA *does* spend a lot of money on R&D, reported to be on average about 17 percent of their large budgets. However, they spend 35 percent, twice as much, on marketing. In addition, the U.S. government, through the NIH (National Institute of Health) and through federal grants for university research, pays for much of the basic work needed to develop chemical molecules that eventually become our medications. Thus, we the taxpayers have already prepaid for part of PhRMA's R&D costs.

In an international contest called Critical Assessment of Structure Prediction on February 6, 2019, one of the leading molecule designers in the world, a multiple previous winner of this competition, was unexpectedly bested by Deep Mind, an artificial intelligence lab owned by Google. Within a few years, the pharmaceutical industry may not be as "burdened" by labor-intensive and costly R&D projects. The machines might do more (see Chapter 1).

In his 1962 book *Capitalism and Freedom,* the esteemed economist Milton Friedman wrote a passage that over the years has influenced many economists: "Few trends could so thoroughly undermine the very foundation of our free society as the acceptance by corporate officials of a social responsibility other than to make as much money for their stockholders as possible."

In an environment of normal economics, such expression may have been reasonable and understandable. Professor Friedman's attitude, the primacy of the unrelenting quest for money, works in many contexts. However, as I have explained (and in seasoned economists' opinions), healthcare is not a normal economic environment.

The drive for profit in an economic sector that has a big gas pedal but weak brakes causes cost explosion. Aside from cost, the values healthcare embraces (for example, the importance of health and happiness) are also diminished by a "Friedman philosophy" that does not encourage expression of socially responsible business impulses when they do not maximize profit.

When I was a medical student in 1967, the cost of a syringe and a vial of epinephrine for use in an emergency allergic situation was probably a few dollars. (The actual cost of the epinephrine and plastic to produce an EpiPen today is probably still very low.) Forty years later, in 2007 when the generic drug manufacturer Mylan obtained the rights to sell the EpiPen, the retail cost was $94. Just ten years later, for no apparent reason save for the desire of Mylan to make more money and the inability of the healthcare market to appropriately apply the brakes on price inflation, the cost rose to $600.

I heard a snippet of an interview with the CEO of Mylan, and I recall her candid response, which shocked me even then: *We have an obligation to make money for our stockholders and raising the price is good business.*

For-profit corporations, like Mylan, do have a fiduciary responsibility to make money for their stockholders. When they raise the price and the market continues to buy and they raise it again, they are in a sense doing what is required to serve the interests of shareholders. But it is simply unfair to give profit a free rein in an environment where the products (medical widgets, pills, EpiPens, hospital rooms, defibrillators, etc.) are so intrinsically important to living a good life that the market does not and cannot hold back the cost.

In our capitalistic society, as we watch the outrageous escalation of the price of pills or an EpiPen (or a hospital room or an insurance premium), too few of us understood that a lot of the problems could be attributed to the failed economics of the free market in healthcare that does not work, and never will work properly.

The pharmaceutical industry, like other special interests, takes advantage of our dysfunctional economics and, in addition, aggressively lobbies politicians to make the playing field even more lopsided in their favor.

Before Obamacare, pharmaceutical corporations did well. With Obamacare, they continued to do well. Following are a few indicators that illuminate both the obesity of their profits, and their callousness.

When human lives are at stake, false advertising or concealment of problems with a medication can have health consequences that can be devastating, causing suffering and perhaps even death. In 2009, Eli Lilly agreed to pay a $1.4 billion fine for inappropriately marketing one of their medications. Later that year, Pfizer paid a $2.3 billion fine to settle a similar issue.

In late October of 2011, British pharmaceutical giant Galaxo-SmithKline agreed to pay a $750 million fine related to the manufacture and distribution of adulterated drugs from a now-closed manufacturing facility in Puerto Rico. Then, on July 3, 2012, it was announced that the company had agreed to pay an additional $3 billion. Two billion represented noncriminal fines related to the marketing of an asthma drug and a few other medications. One billion of the fine was for fraud stemming from promotion of two antidepressants not approved by the FDA, and for hiding adverse safety data related to a diabetes drug.

If pharmaceutical corporations can pay such fines without major hiccups, they are doing very well financially. During the years covered by the $3.75 billion settlement, Galaxo-SmithKline made nearly $28 billion on the sales of the two antidepressants and the one diabetic medication mentioned above.

If the taxpaying public's contribution to R&D through tax support of the National Institutes of Health and federal research grants to universities were appropriately recognized, our medication prices could and should be lower. If we were not politically blocked from negotiating lower prices, as was the case with the Medicare Part D legislation, our medication costs could and should be lower. If the ability to buy the same drugs in other countries had not been aggressively opposed by the political lobbying efforts of Big Pharma, our drug prices could and should be much lower. In effect, American patients pay such inflated prices for their medications that we subsidize patients in other countries whose prices *are* much lower.

I continue to hear politicians and pundits say, "We must find a free market solution." I, too, favor a free market solution, except when the market won't work according to normal economic "law."

We can try whatever healthcare free market solution we want until hell freezes over and it won't work. But I have hope; I think we're waking up. For example, I'm beginning to hear more voices calling for the government to regulate drug prices. But I do not hear any of those voices acknowledging the obvious, the regulation of drug prices is not a free market mechanism; it's socialized. It's exactly how and why prices and costs should and could be restrained across the board with the advent of Medicare.

Without some form or degree of government regulation, drug prices and other medical prices will continue to inflate. This is a why all other nations with wealth and medical sophistication put patients first rather than profit first, and why they regulate healthcare to the financial and health benefit of their economies and citizens.

For the benefit of our senior citizens, as well as many disabled citizens in America, current Medicare already controls many outrageous healthcare charges. With Medicare, where drug prices are concerned, we'd have to rescind the pharmaceutically influenced legislation that prevents Medicare from negotiating the best drug price for patients, but it could be done. Under Medicare, drug companies could still be profitable, but not obscenely profitable.

May your insurance company decide constipation is a pre-existing condition.

– *New Yiddish Sarcasm*

Chapter 12
Private Health Insurance

Over the years, Ronnie and I have been able to afford reasonable albeit expensive insurance. For a while we were somewhat complacent about healthcare insurance, but not anymore.

We've watched as friends and patients, hard-working honorable people, were unable to afford even bad health insurance, or unable to obtain affordable insurance because they had a pre-existing condition. Many years ago, we established a corporation (nonprofit in the absolute sense of the word) to specifically manage the expenses for our group of eight solo practitioners. That corporation allowed us to become a two-person group for healthcare insurance purposes. Thirteen years ago our group of two was dissolved when I took Medicare, forcing Ronnie to apply for an individual private policy to cover her for three and a half years, until she was eligible for Medicare. Although she applied for the same private insurance she'd had for more than ten years, and despite the company's possession of all her health information for that period, the company refused to use the information it had. She had to spend countless hours compiling a new application containing the same information. Eventually, she was able to secure a policy but at increased cost.

By forcing her to reapply as an individual, the insurance company could charge more for a policy that provided less coverage than our two-person "group" policy. The new policy also allowed the insurance company to refuse to pay if it decided that the application was incomplete or erroneous. In other words, the company would profit from any mistake Ronnie made in the application. This type of windfall was disallowed by Obamacare that unfortunately was not yet in effect.

Historically, between World War II and the inception of the Affordable Care Act, a polyglot of different private insurance companies, each with multiple policies, grew like Topsy. Although there are more than 800 health insurance companies in the United States, the largest six control about 50 percent of the US market. Many if not most of these companies offer multiple policies. The resulting array of insurance options is daunting.

For the purpose of demonstrating just how confusing American health insurance can be, I'll describe the different insurance situations of our office associates and their spouses those many years ago. There has been little simplification of the insurance landscape since – perhaps it's even worse.

Ronnie and I were two of the eight independent professionals in our office. At that time, the eight solo practitioners who were working under one roof included five PhD clinical psychologists, one LCSW (licensed clinical social worker), and two MD psychiatrists. Of the six practitioners besides Ronnie and me, five were married. We had three full-time office staff, one of whom was married. So, including spouses there were a total of seventeen adults that comprised that group.

Among these seventeen adults were fourteen different healthcare insurance situations. Two individuals had no insurance, two had similar government coverage (Medicare), and two had health savings accounts (HSA). The eleven other adults each had private insurance policies from different companies with different plans. Upon questioning, of the fifteen adults who had insurance coverage (including Ronnie and me), no one really had a precise understanding of the details of their different plans.

If this diversity had in some way improved the American health landscape that would have been great. However, it did not. Complexity, randomness, confusion, and inconsistency seemed to be the common denominator.

For most, the cost to be insured privately was unduly high; if a less expensive policy could be found, the performance of the insurance was usually poor. Add that to a pattern of insurance churn and change, on average every three to four years, and the picture is even more *meshuge* (Yiddish for crazy).

Before Ronnie and I became eligible for Medicare, we had relatively good private insurance, but the premiums were costing us $2300 per month. While this situation with high premiums is not typical, it is relevant for about 15 percent of Americans.

I am sharing our personal situation to highlight two rarely mentioned Medicare attributes: First, our current blend of government Medicare coverage plus private supplemental insurance is at least the equal and probably superior to the expensive private insurance we previously had; second, Medicare, even with added supplemental policies, often costs less — sometimes by a lot.

When I became eligible for Medicare, my portion of our private health insurance cost $15,600 per year. That annual cost would have undoubtedly increased had I continued the private policy.

My annual cost for Medicare (including supplemental policies) is now about $6,600 per year. Therefore, lowering cost by about $9,000 per year over the twelve years has saved me approximately $117,000 out of pocket.

For the few years before she was eligible for Medicare, and with that new individual private policy, Ronnie paid about $13,200 per year. Ronnie's Medicare cost is also about $6,600 per year. Thus, she saved about $6,600 per year over her eight years on Medicare. Her out-of-pocket cost over that time was reduced by approximately $59,400. Since we both have been on Medicare, compared to what we would have spent in the private insurance market, we have together, out of pocket, saved at least $176,000 of insurance premium costs. Given the fact that I didn't account for the predictable inflation of private insurance premiums over these years, we've probably saved closer to $200,000. Whatever the exact out of pocket savings we experienced, it's a helluva lot.

One day many years ago, I was speaking with one of our receptionists whose job at that time included many hours sorting out insurance coverage for patients. She suggested something she wanted me to include in *Assholistic Healthcare,* the book I was then writing. "Tell them about the big bullies."

"Big bullies?"

"The insurance companies."

I smiled. It struck me that government is often referred to as "Big Brother." Why not refer to the private insurance powerhouses as "Big Bullies"? Indeed, both the private sector and the government can be pretty intrusive; and it was my impression that the private companies were worse. I remember an all too believable snippit of private health insurance humor: The agent told him, "Yes, your policy does cover your falling off the roof, but it doesn't cover your hitting the ground."

Anecdotes are not equivalent to scientific studies, but many of you will feel frustration if not outright anger with the following story. It offers a vivid and unfortunate example of the unintended consequences that can occur when profit trumps principle:

Around the time I am describing, I had a casual conversation with a retired college professor. He mentioned that his wife had passed away a few years earlier. "It was a very sad situation," he told me. "She was being treated successfully for severe rheumatoid arthritis with a very powerful and expensive medication – then our insurance company changed."

"Why?" I asked.

"I don't know; it was something my employer decided."

The new insurance company did not include his wife's arthritis medication in their formulary. The new company covered a different but "equivalent" medication. Their insurance denied an appeal by his wife's physician to make an exception and approve the medication that had been working well. They simply refused.

Without insurance her previous medication would have cost the professor and his wife about a thousand dollars a month out of pocket, so they reluctantly gave in and decided to give the new medication a try. Tragically, she experienced a catastrophic side effect to the new medication and died.

When someone is doing well with a medication, any medication, it is in that person's medical best interest to continue with that medication. Every one of us is different, idiosyncratic, and the particular medication that successfully treats one individual's health problem is not always the same as the medication that will successfully treat another person's similar problem; nor is the best medication for a given individual predictable ahead of time. So, once you find *that* medication, the one that works, it is sometimes not easily replaced by a different medication, however supposedly similar.

The pattern of medication restriction (rationing) by different insurance companies is erratic and can be best understood as a tactic to secure a financial deal to save the insurance company money. This has nothing to do with best patient care. No one could have predicted that the professor's wife would have suffered that rare reaction to the new medication, but the decision to switch her medication was not medically necessary.

Ironically the phrase "not medically necessary" has in the past served as a private insurance euphemism for denying hospitalization, lab testing, imaging, medication, or other medical goods and services. As explained in Chapter 3, there is no question that we have to ration healthcare; we simply can't afford whatever we want. But we should all be alarmed with profit-motivated insurance companies steering the ship. Who is practicing medicine in these cases, the doctor or the insurance company?

Prior to implementation of Obamacare, and

still today, health insurance is for many the medical equivalent of a dowry. When my son Eli and his wife Julia were married in September 2008, they wrote their own vows. As Eli stood with Julia, telling her the reasons he loved her, he brought down the house with his final declaration, "and I love you for your health insurance."

Our close friends Alan and Kathleen were in attendance. Alan, who you met in Chapter 2, was a professor of medicine at the University of Florida; Kathleen is a professional "laughologist" who practices healing through laughter and humor. At the time of Eli and Julia's wedding, Alan and Kathleen had been married five years, but we didn't know it; almost no one did. We were the first of their friends to have the chance to belatedly congratulate them when Eli's quip about Julia's health insurance prompted them to disclose their own story.

Kathleen is very fit and for many years ran almost daily on the beach. One morning, while running on the hard sand, she fell and improbably shattered her elbow. She would need about $50,000 worth of surgery. Kathleen didn't have health insurance.

Kathleen and Alan had been discussing marriage for some time. As a professor, Alan had excellent health insurance that would immediately cover his wife if he married. So, despite the pain, Kathleen said in her usual comedic style, "About that marriage thing, now would be a good time." Once more, the romantic allure of health insurance carried the day. Alan and Kathleen are living happily covered ever after. So is her elbow.

Alan's good private insurance was largely subsidized by the State of Florida through the university. Their marriage was pre-Obamacare, but in addition to information in Chapter 6, it's worth another brief exploration of Obamacare, specifically its relation to private insurance.

Obamacare was designed to help lower-income patients obtain insurance through Medicaid, and also to subsidize the sale of some private insurance (a little like Dr. Halperin's insurance was subsidized by the State of Florida). While Obamacare was gestating, political reality clearly required backing from the insurance industry in order to pass the bill. The insurance companies eventually agreed to support the legislation because they believed their bottom line would be improved with the acquisition of millions of new customers.

Just to be clear and before we explore further, a crucially important public misconception needs to be explained – *there is no such thing as Obamacare insurance.*

The Affordable Care Act simply set up exchanges to sell private insurance; it is the same kind of private insurance we had before Obamacare. Put another way, Obamacare helps some people find private insurance, and helped some people financially by supporting some of the cost. There was, however, no invention of a new kind of insurance; this was just a continuation of the overwhelming and constantly changing panorama of the private insurance cacophony.

Although Obamacare did not create any new insurance policies, it did prohibit the sale of some really cheap but almost useless policies. However, under the Trump administration, the sale of this type of private policy was resurrected, and the policies were just as lousy as they were before Obamacare.

The goal of private insurance corporations is to make money. Obamacare is a hybrid – in part promoting private insurance through exchanges; in part promoting Medicaid. In terms of the private insurance side, because profit comes first and patients second, Obamacare is not likely to restrain the inflating cost of private American healthcare insurance.

Well before Obamacare existed, the cost of private insurance went up and up. The cost of hospital stays, medical devices, and drugs went up and up. The cost of almost everything medical went up and up. This had everything to do with the failure of the free market to restrain costs and just about nothing to do with the Affordable Care Act.

An article in *Money* magazine in late 2016, reflecting a Kaiser Family Foundation study, put it this way: from 2001 to 2006 during the Bush administration, average family health insurance premiums rose 63 percent (pre-Obamacare); from 2006 to 2011 – 31 percent (pre-Obamacare); from 2011 to 2016 – 20 percent (partially with Obamacare).

A couple of years after Obamacare began to operate, the private insurance industry became predictably disgruntled and probably regretted their support. So, after those first few honeymoon years, what did they do? They behaved exactly like private insurance companies always do.

With Obamacare they had to sell less profitable insurance policies that had no caps, that forced acceptance of less profitable patients who had pre-existing conditions, and they also couldn't sell those lousy policies that were very profitable. So, they raised premiums and dropped out of less profitable markets. As I said, they behaved exactly like you would expect profit-making businesses to behave.

In all fairness, private insurance companies are formed to make money for their shareholders; that is their fiduciary responsibility. It might have worked if the market operated as it does in other economic sectors – unfortunately, it does not.

To clarify further (as mentioned in Chapter 4), if we were to permit the sale of all health insurance across state lines, often suggested as a competitive strategy to lower cost, I believe, as with the initial years of Obamacare, cost would at first come down. In all probability, after three to four years of such reduction, as with the Obamacare private insurance scenario, we would again see the cost of insurance gradually increase. Profits are what stockholders demand of most private corporations. After a few years of interstate competition, the insurance market would re-equilibrate and the cost of insurance would rise again.

The special interest corporations in healthcare, definitely including insurance, have been operating in an economic marketplace with loaded dice; the playing field is tilted, and patients are at a disadvantage. The human desire for good health is so basic, so intense that demand doesn't let up no matter how many pills or treatments are offered. Remember – big gas pedal, tiny brakes. We are beginning to learn that overall function of the market is not quite what it's cracked up to be; but this abject failure of the free market in the healthcare sector is truly unusual.

Compared to private health insurance, government health insurance (Medicare) has lower premiums, no restrictions on pre-existing conditions, no caps, and generally much smaller deductibles to satisfy before your insurance begins to pay. These advantages have already been baked into the Medicare cake. Over time, an evolving Medicare would have the potential for even more improvement. I believe it would be easier for physicians to negotiate intelligent change with the single-headed Medicare dragon than the distracting, ever-changing, multi-headed private insurance dragon. Cost savings would come from a control of pricing, from administrative efficiency, from a potential reduction of defensive medicine, and more emphasis on prevention. Subsequent chapters of *Patients Before Profits* are devoted to these issues.

Treatment without prevention is simply unsustainable.

– Bill Gates

Chapter 13
The Power of Prevention: From Sick Care to Healthcare

I completed my residency in psychiatry in 1978 and immediately opened a private office in San Francisco. Although my practice went well, I was missing general medicine. At that time, I also had some concerns about psychiatry itself. So surprisingly in 1980, I closed my psychiatry practice and moved east to Bennington, Vermont.

Deciding to integrate my psychiatric training to enhance a family practice, I joined two family practitioners in Vermont. Ronnie joined the practice as a psychologist since she had received her PhD shortly before our move.

Bennington is a small community with a population of about 15,000, with the surrounding population numbering around 45,000. The arrival of a young professional couple in town was enough to warrant an article in the local newspaper. Within a few days of the publication of that article, we received a call from Dale Guldbrandsen, who was then an executive with the local Stanley Tools manufacturing plant. He asked if we had an interest in what is now called wellness medicine; we did. He invited us to visit the factory, and that meeting turned out to be the beginning of a lifelong friendship.

Toward the end of our meeting, Dale asked whether we might be willing to visit to the factory on a regular basis and speak to employees about health. Way ahead of the curve, Dale recognized that the cost of health for business was growing rapidly. He explained that in 1977, General Motors had spent more on employee healthcare than on steel. It made sense to him to educate the Stanley workers to live healthier.

Dale, Ronnie, and I eventually began a small company, New England Preventive Medicine. We developed educational relationships with a number of small companies in rural Vermont, Massachusetts, and New York.

Dale also became the Chairman of the Vermont Natural Resources Council (VNRC). He eventually left Stanley, met and later married another friend of ours, Sally Dodge, and became an independent organizational consultant.

The Dodge family owned a substantial farming and ranching operation in southern Vermont, which Sally ran. Long before the concept was widely known, she became a pioneer in Vermont's organic farming movement, one of the earliest in the U.S. Years later, but still well ahead of her time, she also drove the local farm-to-table movement.

Over the many years of our friendship, a lot of conversation crossed the transom about the transformation of our healthcare system. Placing more emphasis on preventing healthcare problems made more sense than our current "sick care" emphasis of addressing a health problem after it begins. (Sally and Dale are co-founders of The Patients Party.)

Preventive medicine embraces many aspects of living. One aspect is related to the exponential explosion of knowledge and technology that will be the subject of the last chapter. For the past century, our physical environment, including water, land, and air, has been subjected to an onslaught of chemical molecules that didn't previously exist.

Unless, like Sally and Dale, you happen to be an obsessive organic farm-to-table devotee, your human diet is probably awash with some contaminants or unhealthy chemicals. How many of us live in areas that are particularly exposed to an avalanche of soil toxins, along with air or water pollution? Also, how many of us live in food deserts, having no stores nearby that offer the kinds of foods that are intrinsically healthier, let alone organically grown? And if organic food is available, how many of us can afford it?

Remember also, it's not just your exposure to toxins that counts. How many of us are more vulnerable to such toxic intrusion? Your personal genetic idiosyncratic vulnerability to these chemicals is very significant but at this time not easy to assess.

The Dodge-Guldbrandsen duo are particularly annoying in restaurants. They are so knowledgeable about chemical contamination that they cannot refrain from engaging in a very detailed conversation about food sourcing with the waitress, chef, owner, or even other patrons. It can be embarrassing, but the more I have come to know, the more I understand why they are so passionate. I'll turn to cats to create clarity about modern food pollution.

If you have a cat, here's a question: Is she behaving different lately? If so, take your cat to the veterinarian and have her thyroid checked.

According to an article in *The New York Times,* feline thyroid problems, once rare, have risen to epidemic proportions. The cause is supposedly the increasing use of certain pesticides and other soil contaminants that have infiltrated commercial cat food, leading to thyroid consequences that couldn't have been predicted. I wonder how many of us are already "sick cats" and don't know it.

Fifty-plus years ago, when I was in medical school, there was little emphasis on prevention. While there are more opportunities to explore prevention than there were then, it's not necessarily easy to change longstanding behavior, or to protect the environment. And it is still much easier for physicians to generate income by treating sickness rather than promoting wellness.

As wonderful as is modern technology, when it comes to improving the overall health of our nation and saving money, MRIs, PETs, robots, and genome analysis pale in comparison to the societal impact and potential power of preventive/wellness medicine. Despite the controversial current opinions in our pandemic environment, vaccination for many human illnesses is a preventive strategy responsible for saving millions of lives and changing the trajectory of human health.

There is no question that we need treatment when we're sick. But as Bill Gates recently said, "Treatment without prevention is simply unsustainable." Cats and humans could eat less contaminated food, inhale fewer air pollutants, drink cleaner water, be more physically active, and treat certain chronic illnesses more aggressively using both sick care and health enhancing strategies. *The Blood Sugar Solution*, published in 2012 authored by Dr. Mark Hyman, supports this. The best preventive treatment is what he calls "intensive lifestyle therapy." Dr. Hyman identifies a core problem: "No one profits from lifestyle medicine, so it is not part of medical education or practice. Prevention should be the foundation of our healthcare system, but doctors ignore it because they get paid to dispense medication and perform surgery. They should be paid to develop and conduct practice-based and community programs in sustainable lifestyle change."

All nutritional issues raised by prevention involve chemicals. All foods we ingest, organic or not, are chemicals. The toxins in some of those foods are chemicals. In addition to the chemicals produced by pharmaceutical corporations, all vitamins, minerals, herbs, and other "nutraceuticals" we find in health food stores are chemicals. Depending on your unique body, some chemicals are more healthful for *you* than others. You may be far better off taking a strong medication that causes you no side effects, than ingesting the organic chemical known as "peanut" to which you are allergic.

Private insurance plans change hands frequently. A private insurance company generally has about three and a half to four years of "medical responsibility" for a person's healthcare; then that person switches or is switched to another policy. Because of a shortsighted, profit-driven, shareholder-friendly attitude, private health insurance companies have historically expressed little enthusiasm for prevention.

The Affordable Care Act recognized this shortsightedness as well as the long-term value of prevention. Obamacare does direct insurance companies to provide preventive services with free examinations, mammograms, and other evaluations. However, these enhancements are just a start.

While writing *The Healing of America,* T.R. Reid interviewed his namesake John Reid, who was then chief of the British National Health Service. In comparing his system with our system, John Reid explained clearly why a universal government-based plan, such as the one in Great Britain, paid so much attention to prevention. Simply put, in England the government is financially responsible for healthcare costs from birth to death. Keeping people healthy and well reduces doctor and hospital visits and saves a ton of money. Saving money is a great incentive. I believe the motivation to aggressively fund preventive medicine would bloom in America if we had a single-payer government insurance program like Medicare.

A massive study by the RAND Corporation during the seventies and early eighties found that simply spending more money on healthcare, as we do in America, does not always lead to the best health outcomes. Better outcomes are more likely to be tied to better quality of care and to preventive strategies that can range from outlawing or limiting use of potentially toxic chemicals, to educating about lifestyle choices that some of us make.

Amongst legal chemicals that wreak health and economic havoc in America are alcohol, tobacco, and sugar. George Washington imposed a whiskey tax. Later came tax on tobacco. A tax on sugar consumption was originally included in the Affordable Care Act. The food and beverage industry, also a special interest where healthcare is concerned, reportedly spent nearly $60 million dollars lobbying Congress to remove the sugar tax from the final version of the bill. They were successful.

Although the sugar tax failed, many economic conservatives and wellness advocates welcomed the ACA's sensitivity to prevention and its cost-saving power. Had that one-cent-per-ounce tax on the consumption of sugary products been included in Obamacare, it was projected to generate about $13 billion in annual tax revenues. Also projected was an additional $17 billion saved in healthcare costs by reducing the incidence and severity of illnesses such as diabetes, heart disease, and stroke over ten years.

We all have the right to enjoy the pleasure of food, to smoke or drink alcohol, or not exercise, as long as it does not infringe on the rights or safety of others. Inevitably, however, some of these behaviors, like smoking or excessive use of alcohol before driving, may cause harm to others. And some of these behaviors absolutely do impact overall health costs.

Preventively addressing chronic medical illness is another powerful strategy. I'll share a story of one small city in North Carolina that demonstrates just how patients benefit and money is saved when preventive medicine is given its due.

I live in Northeast Florida, and many of my friends travel to Asheville, North Carolina to spend time enjoying cooler weather. According to the *Journal of the American Pharmaceutical Association,* years ago (March 2003) Asheville conducted a very interesting study related to diabetic employees.

Even with its relatively small number of city employees, each diabetic individual on Asheville's payroll was costing the city $7,000 per year above and beyond the medical costs of non-diabetic employees. Not burdened with the political intrigues of state or national health planning, Asheville's city government was free to pursue a course of treatment and education based on logical evidence-based principles of preventive care. The patients in the program were informed and agreed with the plan.

The Asheville Plan did away with prescription formularies for these diabetic patients. Instead, selecting medications was left completely to the discretion of the physicians. All prescribed brand or generic medications were provided free of cost to any diabetic employee who agreed to follow a doctor's plan of treatment. If insurance wouldn't pay, the city did. To support compliance with treatment, each of these employees was required to attend a diabetes education program, with instructors paid by the city. Finally, the pharmacists were paid extra, also at city expense, to interview each employee in the test group every time the employee requested a medication refill. If the pharmacist concluded that an employee was not following the doctor's treatment plan, the employee was required to report for an immediate physician's visit before any further medication was dispensed. The physicians cooperated as well.

Despite providing free brand or generic medication for each employee, and despite paying for the hundreds of pharmacist interviews during the five-year study, Asheville realized average savings of more than $9,000 per diabetic employee in direct medical costs. Above and beyond these savings, Asheville realized an additional $18,000 per year in recovered productivity – fewer sick days for their diabetic employees. Preventive medicine works for the economy and the family. Being well is far less expensive than being ill.

The productivity and financial loss to our economy because of illness is profound. Of equal if not greater importance, preventive medicine works for patients because quality of life is improved if you're healthy.

With a modern version of Medicare and a government naturally incentivized to reduce healthcare costs, primary care physicians could be financially empowered to become strong health advocates and teach prevention and wellness, and we definitely need to boost the ranks of PCPs.

Effective profitable practice of prevention in primary care medicine is *not* unrealistic. Dr. Roy Hinman is profitably practicing the kind of preventive care that includes both aggressive treatment of existing medical problems and lifestyle education that is such an intrinsic part of prevention.

A few years ago, I had lengthy discussions with Dr. Hinman, whose family practice offices in and around Jacksonville continue to thrive. His story is neither common nor presented as the model for the future. But it does demonstrate that quality prevention can reward physicians financially while lowering overall healthcare cost.

Roy is a natural leader and administrator. He is also blessed with enormous energy. A major insurance company identified his practice as being particularly efficient. They made him an offer he decided not to refuse. Based on transparency-enhancing demographic research, the insurance company knew the projected annual per capita cost of care for a local group of approximately 10,000 patients covered by that company. Hinman would be paid a fixed amount to manage this large group of patients. If he spent less than the projected amount, he would keep the profit. If he spent more, he would lose money. (Medicare patients represented a substantial portion of this group.) It includes both aggressive treatment of existing medical problems and lifestyle education that Dr. Hyman refers to.

This sort of agreement is known as "capitation" and in my view has generally not had a happy history. Some physicians who have entered into these contracts, consistent unfortunately with medicine as a business, try to restrict expenditure as much as possible, limiting services for their patients, and making more profit by keeping more of the money they were paid in advance; this was not Roy's strategy.

In addition to his energy and managerial skill, he

first and foremost utilized the real power of prevention and wellness in a meaningful way to lead his patients to more health and less illness. He believed that preventive medicine would drive his cost down; he was correct.

Dr. Hinman's group practice employs other physicians and physician extenders (physician assistants and nurse practitioners). These professionals receive a base salary, not fee-for-service, but can earn bonuses or profit share based on the quality of their performance. They were specifically not required to see large volumes of patients.

Roy explained that one provision of the agreement was that "changes in a patient's care should first be in the best interest of the patient, and second should save money." These objectives are not mutually exclusive.

Hinman and his partners address each patient's chief complaint at each office visit. But they also focus relentlessly on lifestyle and on every patient's blood pressure, weight, smoking, cholesterol, and sugar level – no matter what the presenting complaint. He knew that problems arising from lifestyle-related ailments often go undiagnosed; and if they are diagnosed, they are not always treated aggressively. His office walls were plastered with posters, often humorous, regaling the benefits of not smoking and of losing weight. His bookcase shelves displayed globs of disgusting looking fake fat to graphically illustrate to patients what their insides look like.

His patients were at first confused: "I just came in for a toe problem, Doc."

"I'll take care of your toe, but your toe problem won't kill you – your cholesterol might. Let's find out what that is."

And so it went.

Today, after years of experience with the preventive medicine/lifestyle change model, his patients do understand and are pleased with the results. "Our plan is working. Our patients, by any measure, are far less ill than a similar group in which doctors are rushing through one patient after another, putting out fires rather than focusing on long-term health."

While visiting one of his practices with him he mentioned to me that the average LDL (low density lipoprotein) amongst his patients was 77mg/Dl. The target level for this "bad" cholesterol is below 100mg/

Dl. Many patients do not achieve that.

We walked into the area where patient records were stored (they're now computerized), and he invited me to pull ten charts at random and calculate the average LDL cholesterol. I laughed, wandered around grabbing ten charts at random, and made the calculation. Ridiculously, the average was – you guessed it – 77 mg/Dl.

I'm certain that wouldn't happen every time, but the point is this: because he and his physicians, nurse practitioners, and physicians' assistants relentlessly pursued relevant preventive issues with every patient at every visit, they were achieving important results.

Roy told me that physicians in his group see their Medicare patients more than eight times a year. He says most Medicare patients in traditional practices are seen between three and four times a year. "We try to help before the problem is out of control. Prevention begins sooner and costs less than illness treatment, so preventive lifestyle strategies improve health and save money."

He also told me that he may hospitalize a patient sooner than is the case in other practices, and not seek to cut their hospital stay to a minimum. "When one of our patients is developing a problem, we tend not to wait to hospitalize; we do it sooner than later. And we don't rush patients out of the hospital prematurely. We want them to really recover, and to not be re-hospitalized."

Here's the irony – because his patients have become healthier, most cost savings realized by his practice result from much lower utilization of the hospital overall. His practice substantially improves patient outcomes *and* saves money.

If Hinman's group made it difficult for patients to be seen, or cut corners on their care to save money, their patients would be sicker and ultimately cost more to finally treat. At that point, his group's financial goose would be cooked. But his goose is just fine. The Hinman goose is indeed a rare bird – a situation in which the healthier your patients are the more money you make.

According to Harvard faculty member Dr. Vivian Lee, writing in her comprehensive book *The Long Fix*, perhaps the pioneer goose of this type flew the coop in the early 1990s in Miami. Dr. Chris Chen and his wife, his nonphysician office manager, began to care for sick and elderly Cuban immigrants who were not insured, by paying attention to healthy living and other prevention strategies. They improved health and drove costs down so successfully that they secured contracts with Medicare Advantage plans and the Chen clinics proliferated.

Taking a broad systems approach, Dr. Lee diagnoses the core American healthcare problem:

> "The root cause of this crisis is the fee-for-service system: we pay for each pill, echocardiogram, laboratory test, or operation regardless of whether it makes people healthier. Our system rewards action, not better health outcomes. It encourages overtreatment and specialty care at the expense of prevention and primary care. For example, every headache or backache warrants an MRI in a fee-for-service world, and every episode of chest pain (even if it's just indigestion) justifies a coronary angiogram. This is *the* fundamental flaw of American healthcare."

Our Medicare, despite significant cost-saving measures, is still hampered in applying a more potent preventive cast to America's healthcare because it is inextricably tied to the much more inflationary private insurance. If Medicare were to become the true universal primary-payer health insurance system for the United States, prevention might flourish. As suggested above by John Reid, the former head of the British Health System, saving money responsibly in healthcare by promoting more prevention becomes a priority when an economy has major responsibility for the health of all of its citizens from birth to death. This is exactly why I believe the Medicare of our future "will not be your grandmother's Medicare." Wellness has more impact the longer it's practiced. No doubt a newly designed Medicare, not profit-motivated but certainly motivated by issues of cost savings, could be significantly more invested in prevention and wellness across America at every age.

There have been many studies of financial benefit to companies who invest in health programs like those we developed in the early eighties with New England Preventive Medicine. In 2010, the Harvard Business

Review reported on a large study of a program at Johnson and Johnson and reported that the company saved $250 million on healthcare costs between 2002 and 2008; the return on investment (ROI) was $2.71 for every dollar spent. A few years later, a study of a polyglot of different studies reported savings, but more from disease prevention than lifestyle management. However, not all lifestyle benefits to patients can be measured just by money saved.

The prestigious Institute of Medicine clearly recognized that the benefits of Wellness Programs often extend well beyond the mighty dollar. They concluded that workplace well-being may include important benefits such as social cohesion of work teams. However, monetizing the value of the pride, trust, and respect that comes from being actively engaged in the company's health and wellness program may not be possible. Yet, these factors carry inherent value to organizations.

In the paragraph above are two words that represent a power element in the world of preventive medicine: *social cohesion*. Whether it's at work or relationships with family and friends, our human connections on a day-to-day basis are the most important element in your overall health.

Those of you who believe that the primary organ involved in the regulation of human emotion is the brain are partially correct. I say partially because there's a lot more to it. How often have you heard that someone has a "broken heart"? Or how often have you said you had a "gut feeling"? We now understand that input from both the heart and the GI system, including the microbiome, contributes much to our emotional environment. And if you were also to say, "They just broke up and he is experiencing a lot of immune system ache," you might be correct as well. Human emotion is indeed complex.

It might not be surprising, for instance, if a heart doctor were to make a significant contribution to the understanding of our emotional world. Thus, it was that twenty-one years ago a cardiologist by the name of Dean Ornish wrote a groundbreaking book entitled *Love and Survival.* Dr. Ornish begins with the following: "This book is based on a simple but powerful idea: Our survival depends on the healing power of love, intimacy, and relationships.

Physically. Emotionally. Spiritually. As individuals, as communities, as a culture, perhaps even as a species."

As a young man, Dan Buettner traveled the world by bicycle. Both as an adventurer and scientist, he made observations about healthy living and developed his concept of Blue Zones (See *Blue Zones and Blue Zones of Happiness)* as areas where people lived longer and seemed generally healthier and happier, characteristics that reflect the essential goals of prevention and life.

He identified a few areas of the world where these fortunate circumstances were prevalent: Sardinia, an island off the coast of Italy; Okinawa, islands off the coast of Japan; Loma Linda, California, about sixty miles east of Los Angeles; the village of Hojancha in Costa Rica; finally, the Greek island of Ikaria, located about thirty miles off the western coast of Turkey.

Buettner and associates identified nine common factors that characterized these areas. The common factors were in no way identical between the locations, but the core lifestyle issues were always present.

Communities in the United States and in other areas around the world are trying to emulate these characteristics and bring healthier, happier lives to their neighbors.

I strongly encourage those of you interested in this area to pursue your own research. For now, I'll simply oversimplify and distill the nine elements into three issues of key relevance. First, pay strong attention to your social relationships by spending time with loved ones, friends, and family. Take time to talk and laugh every day if possible. Second, take care of your body with good food and lots of physical activity, not necessarily using high technology. Just do it. Third, infuse your existence with purpose and passion – not necessarily writing the great American novel or developing new sources of energy, although that would be fine – and with aspects of your life interests that hold special meaning for you.

We need our sick care system, the blossoming medical science of putting out and controlling healthcare fires. But we absolutely need more emphasis on health.

Eubie Blake, a jazz pianist and a Medicare recipient, was interviewed at the age of 108 regarding his remarkable health. He acknowledged that during his long life he smoked, drank, and chased women.

He then famously said, "If I had known I was going to live this long, I would have taken much better care of myself." Wellness and preventive medicine might not make a major difference for a few of us. But for most of us, it would.

A nickel ain't worth a dime anymore.

– Yogi Berra

Chapter 14
Improving the Health of Your Wallet

Thousands of doctors who support Physicians for a National Health Program (PNHP) agree that our patients and our economy would be far better off with Medicare. The relative economic success of the other nation's healthcare systems, and the economic wastefulness of ours, is not an abstraction. PNHP has harvested an enormous amount of information supporting their (and my) position.

Modern Medicare need not be your grandmother's

Medicare. It need not perpetuate the problems of unfairness and political influence that are visible in our current Medicare. Those problems include legislation that prohibits negotiating with drug companies for better prices, and the practice of paying expensive hospitals more than less expensive outpatient facilities for comparable services. Also, as noted, I believe a significant amount of cost reduction and health improvement would result from prevention and universal coverage.

Einstein said it best: "One should not pursue goals that are easily achieved. One must develop an instinct for what one can barely achieve through one's greatest efforts." We can't outspend special interests, but we can use the benefit of a more informed electorate with better understanding of healthcare issues to guide our election choices according to what's best for patients, and not what's best for business. It is then that our votes become more powerful than special interest dollars.

What might we accomplish if we do graduate from Obamacare to a more compassionate Medicare?

Here's my idealized list:

- Provision of true *universal* insurance coverage – health insurance coverage of every baby, child, indeed every American from birth to death
- Dramatic reduction of healthcare profiteering
- Reduction of U.S. per capita healthcare cost
- Elimination of bankruptcy based on medical costs
- Simplification of healthcare funding
- Relieve business of the administrative burden, and some of the financial burden of providing healthcare insurance
- Elimination of all pre-existing condition exclusions
- Elimination of annual or lifetime caps
- Provision of a robust foundation for continuing and enhancing healthcare research, preventive medicine, and public health planning research (reference the current pandemic)
- Change the malpractice environment, improve the doctor-patient relationship, and reduce defensive medicine costs
- Elevation of American healthcare to a more deserved position of overall excellence

Assume that your personal all-inclusive "healthcare tax" represents not only the explicit taxes that you contribute to healthcare, but also everything else you spend on healthcare for you and your family. When you add our historically lower (than some "socialized" counties) government-based healthcare taxes to our high-priced private insurance premiums, deductibles, copays, drug prices, and caps on medical expenses, our personal healthcare "taxes" are quite high.

By way of contrast, countries with high government healthcare taxes have far lower out-of-pocket health costs than we do. Even though they pay higher healthcare taxes, they generally don't have high premiums, high deductibles, high copays, or caps. In addition, the cost of medical procedures, hospitals, drugs, and medical devices is often much lower. So, the amount we contribute to healthcare that we call a tax may be less than the tax in Norway or Great Britain, but add our lower taxes to our far more expensive out-of-pocket "taxes" and many of our healthcare wallets are bleeding green.

Beginning this writing journey, I did not understand how much the out-of-pocket expenditures of many individual patients and families would be reduced with Medicare. I also did not understand that Medicare could save money for the entire American economy.

Remember that the per capita cost of Medicare for a sixty-five-year old is far less than the current overall U.S. per capita cost. If adoption of Medicare over time eventually leads to Medicare for All , even though we would add a lot of patients, most would be much younger, healthier, and far less expensive to cover than our current group of elderly and disabled.

Predictably, the combined premiums and taxes paid by the very large group of younger Medicare enrollees would likely be a good deal for Medicare. And at the same time, younger recipients would pay less for Medicare than for equivalent private insurance.

Thus, with Medicare, it is even possible that per capita healthcare cost would drop. This absolutely will not happen with Obamacare or any other American healthcare system that continues putting profits before patients. If we don't accept reasonable government involvement in healthcare, and we continue to pretend that our dysfunctional healthcare free market will steer our ship straight, no way in hell will we ever achieve a reduction of per capita healthcare expense in America.

I'll try to specifically project the ways in which Medicare for All might save that money. The Congressional Budget Office (CBO), with all its resources, struggles with these financial projections. I obviously don't have CBO's resources, so my strategy for not making a fool of myself is to be ultra-conservative with my financial projections. What I include to support the notion that we really can save money will be so ferociously limited that it will not nearly reflect the amount of savings I believe we can ultimately achieve. So much so that it will be difficult to consider my projections overly optimistic or unrealistic, except maybe on the low side.

First of all, my Medicare savings tally will not include any amount resulting from the theoretical, and perhaps idealistic, malpractice reform I suggested. Also, I will not include the potentially large reductions of the defensive medical savings by covering physicians' malpractice that I've spoken of previously. Not to say I believe we can't accomplish this, only that it will take substantial innovation.

Princeton economist Uwe Reinhart commented that in general, as you now know, Medicare pays much less than those ridiculously inflated prices charged by hospitals. Yet most hospitals whose patient population is predominantly Medicare do reasonably well. However, I will not include the likely savings because of Medicare's reduction of inflated prices paid for hospitalizations, medications, or other services and supplies.

Some might argue that the ultimate savings from defensive medicine, the reduction of payments to hospitals, should be included. I agree, but in order to maintain my economic conservatism, I won't do it.

Others might also argue that the reduction of drug prices, and the more aggressive practice of preventive medicine could eventually represent the bulk of cost saving. That might be, but I'm still not including these sources in my tally.

My economic conservatism goes even further. I will not be adding the potential cost savings of all but one of the items below; even then, the amount I include will be an underestimate of the generally accepted potential cost savings.

Medicaid now covers more people than Medicare. Although it varies from state to state, across the United States about two-thirds of Medicaid expenditure is for direct patient care. The rest of Medicaid expense supports long-term care for the elderly and disabled. So, over time Medicare could eventually take over the medical part of Medicaid (and maybe eventually long-term care).

Over time we could also eliminate the need for the Children's Health Insurance Program. Medicare could automatically cover the more than eight million American children currently insured by CHIP.

Eliminating these programs would not eliminate the medical costs of caring for these patients; the costs and the funds to run them already exist, so the money would be shifted to Medicare. However, the administrative costs to run Medicare, as opposed to Medicaid and CHIP programs are lower, so we'd save money. Conservatively, we might actually save billions in yearly administrative expense by shifting these programs. Again, none of these potential savings are included in my savings tally.

Workers compensation is another interesting

story. Born in the nineteenth century, regulations are cumbersome, and costs are high. Under Obamacare, even with the mandate, not everyone would have insurance and workers compensation would be still necessary for some people. However, the medical costs of workers compensation could be eliminated if a Medicare for All program covering everybody was established.

In studies done by the University of Massachusetts, potential annual savings from elimination of workers compensation medical costs are in the range of $50 billion. Medicare would also greatly simplify the medical process for covering injured workers. Nevertheless, in my quest to be egregiously conservative and not overestimate, I will also not include the projected $50 billion in savings.

Medicare Advantage represents another politically induced kick in our financial gut and should not be confused with straight Medicare. For some patients, I think of it as Medicare "Disadvantage."

Medicare Advantage is essentially a hybrid product in which Medicare insurance is managed by private insurance companies that focus first on making a buck and is not as cost efficient, or in some ways as fair, as basic Medicare. In 2004, legislation that allowed Medicare Advantage plans to *risk adjust* was expanded. This means that Medicare Advantage, unlike straight Medicare, is allowed to avoid taking patients who cost more. Risk adjustment, is essentially *denial because of pre-existing conditions.* Strangely, by allowing this, Congress mandated that our government not only pay these private insurance companies management fees to run the "Advantage" plans, but also regular straight Medicare would now by default have to disproportionately cover the care of the more costly and sicker patients with pre-existing conditions that Medicare Advantage was allowed *not* to cover.

Medicare Advantage may provide perks, like coverage for some eyewear, dental work, and hearing aids. It may also include direct financial perks like lowering copays and deductibles while also lowering the amount of the Medicare premium that is deducted each month from your Social Security check. This is good.

But Advantage also limits patients to certain physicians and hospital networks. You can't just choose any doctor like you can with straight Medicare. Finally, Medicare Advantage also restricts coverage for certain medical problems, compared to straight Medicare.

If you are healthy and are unlikely to become ill, Medicare Advantage might be a good deal. But God forbid you become really ill.

According to Physicians for a National Health Program, by paying fees to the insurance companies as well as the healthcare costs, and by allowing Medicare Advantage to enroll primarily healthier seniors, the government overpays Medicare Advantage by as much as $3,000 per patient per year. If all of these "advantaged" patients had straight Medicare, PNHP estimates the government would save $30 billion in healthcare.

With straight Medicare we could create our own individually designed "Advantage" by purchasing supplemental policies in the private insurance market, although at higher expense. It should be noted that job loss in the private insurance industry, something that I believe must be considered, would be buffered by both Advantage and supplemental insurance, both of which support continuation of some private insurance employment. Thus, even though we might lower per capita cost I am not advocating the elimination of Advantage plans.

In sum, I am not including the billions in savings from much reduced Medicare payments for hospitals, physicians, or drugs. Nor do I include cost savings of prevention or defensive medicine, and I don't include efficiency benefits with workers compensation, CHIP, Medicaid, or Medicare Advantage.

I hope you're now curious as to what I am including in my extremely conservative savings tally. Only one item: improved administrative efficiency for managing Medicare overall, but only $250 billion annually and not the $450 billion that many comfortably project. Still, over ten years this alone is $2.5 trillion. With profit-driven Obamacare, costs over ten years per capita cost will rise. With Medicare, cost might come down, if that is what we intend.

What worries some of my colleagues about Medicare is that physicians would have less power if we were under the government's thumb. I don't agree. There is a consensus that getting doctors to work together is often like herding cats. Individual physicians – and even many organized medical groups – do not have significant leverage when negotiating with the multiheaded dragon that is private insurance.

In our current environment, physician focus, already distracted by the increasing blizzard of computerized private insurance company paperwork requirements, will be further whiplashed by the constantly shifting provisions of different private group and individual policies. Medicare would certainly go a long way in making the American health landscape simpler administratively and because of that, more economically efficient.

When Medicare is the insurance of the land, negotiations between Medicare and physicians is likely to be more focused and effective. The Center for Medicare and Medicaid Services (CMS) proposed reduced availability of some antidepressant medications in 2015 and some antipsychotic medications in 2016. Doctors practicing in my specialty and other interested parties thought this was "insane," so we rose up, making our voices heard; the Medicare decisions were reversed.

Is there any hard evidence that my overall speculations about actually lowering healthcare costs might be correct? Absolutely. *All* other nations of wealth and medical sophistication chose Medicare for All or some other form of government ownership or control; by many measures all of their health systems perform better than ours and cost a lot less. That's an enormous amount of evidence-based research.

Over the years of my career, I've been introduced to "acronym optimism." I've seen many iterations of healthcare delivery touted as the potential cure for our healthcare woes: prepaid group practice (PGP), preferred provider organizations (PPO), health maintenance organizations (HMO), managed care (MC), medical homes (MH), patient-centered medical homes (PCMH), health savings accounts (HSA), consumer-directed care (CDC), and now accountable care organizations (ACO). I regret to say that as far as fixing healthcare, most of these programs haven't amounted to a hill of beans (AHOB).

Every man, woman, and child in our country should be able to access the health care they need regardless of their income.

– *Bernie Sanders*

Chapter 15
Universal Medicare: Make American Healthcare Compassionate

A new kind of human creative ability seemed to emerge for the first time about 70,000 years ago. The anthropological record suggests that the ability to project productive ideas into a new infinity called the imagination developed at this time. Speculation is that before then, despite having other kinds of cleverness, no human species had this advantage.

For some reason, only we *Homo sapiens* received this gift. Every human being on the face of this earth

– no matter what the color of your skin, whether tall or short, whether you're black, brown, Asian, native American or white, whether your eyes are blue, brown, grey, hazel, or golden – is a member of the *Homo sapiens* tribe. No other human species remains. Perhaps other humans disappeared because having such a gift of mind conferred a remarkable survival advantage, but in truth no one really knows why.

Collectively, as we members of this tribe rocket intellectually, I pray that our gifts will eventually allow us to place more emphasis on compassion than conflict. In these stressful times, I hope human value of health itself will animate the process of healthcare reform in America to embrace kindness and resilience more than power and partisanship. Otherwise, the continuation of politics as we recently know it may lead to our downfall.

Perhaps we patients will begin to hear a different and more positive perspective about intelligent change rather than political cockamamie. This of course would include understanding that Medicare is realistic, cost saving, and health enhancing -- and that the hybrid socialism already widely entrenched in the United

States is quite different than that in old Germany, Russia, the Eastern Bloc, or even modern England, and will not cause ecumenical poisoning in America.

Although the term "single-payer system" is useful and widely applied, in the strictest sense there is no such thing as a single-payer system. I have yet to find an example of a system anywhere in which some patients, especially those who have wealth, do not purchase some of their care outside the parameters of what's available in their country.

For example, in England where most physicians work for the government, there has long been private care available on Harley Street in London, and elsewhere. And there's always barter. To a greater or lesser extent, in one way or another, some sort of exception insinuates itself into all the so-called single-payer models. With Medicare for All and other universal systems, single-payer would be better described as "primary payer."

As you may have noticed, I've used these labels interchangeably. After World War II when a lot of modern healthcare rebooted, our expectation that a market-driven system would work was understandable.

As I mentioned above, after years of trying to understand why this hasn't worked, why our costs are so high and our overall performance so low, the realization that there was a problem with the market itself was almost a shock. It is understandable that most of our public figures were utterly convinced that we could fix healthcare with market-based principles, but we cannot.

I have little doubt that if any of these public figures read this book, some would at first be sure that I'm wrong. And perhaps they are correct. But for now, until proven otherwise, continued belief in the delusion that the market works in healthcare, or that healthcare can be fixed by making typical market adjustments, is simply unfair to patients and to the American economy.

I've recently been feeling much less alone in my questioning of free market idolatry. Other market critics with voices far more educated and erudite than mine are gradually creating a chorus. Concerns are beginning to surface (see Chapter 3).

In his 2015 book *Misbehaving*, Richard Thaler, Nobel Prize winner in economics, did not explicitly address the healthcare economics issues that we've explored in *Patients Before Profits*, but he absolutely understands that American patients appropriately misbehave. People don't deal with decisions in healthcare as though they are robots; we have emotional flesh and blood in the game.

That our need and demand for healthcare is insatiable is the reason that economics is a *social* science, inevitably linking less predictable human emotion with the more precisely predictable science of mathematics. Mr. Thaler writes: "You know, and I know, that we do not live in a world of Econs [economists]. Adam Smith, the father of modern economic thinking, explicitly acknowledged this fact. Before writing his magnum opus *The Wealth of Nations*, he wrote another book devoted to the topic of human "passions," a word that does not appear in any economics textbook. [It's as though] Econs do not have passions; they are cold blooded optimizers. Think of Mr. Spock in *Star Trek*."

In his panoramic 2015 book *Sapiens*, Yuval Noah Harari says this:

"Ardent capitalists tend to argue that capital should

> be free to influence politics, but politics should not be allowed to influence capital. …In its extreme form, [absolute] belief in the free market is as naïve as belief in Santa Claus. There is simply no such thing as a market free of all political bias."

In 2018, Robert Kuttner's book *Can Democracy Survive Global Capitalism?* was heralded by Robert Reich (former Secretary of Labor and current Professor of Public Policy at the University of California, Berkeley), who wrote these words:

> "Democracies govern nations, while global capitalism runs the world. Robert Kuttner provides a clear-eyed, intellectually riveting account of how the inevitable tensions between the two have fueled neo-fascist nationalism here and abroad, and why the response must be a new progressive populism rooted in democracy and social justice."

Reimagining Capitalism: How the Greatest System Ever Conceived (And Its Billionaires) Need To Change by Randall Lane, published in the March 31, 2019 edition of Forbes magazine, reminded us that B.C.

Forbes, who founded the magazine in 1917, said clearly and right out of the gate that "business was originated to produce happiness, not to pile up millions."

Perhaps because the capitalism of today has to some degree abandoned the more socially conscious vision of the elder Forbes in the early twentieth century, today "just 56 percent of Americans say they have a positive image of capitalism." Indeed, among those currently aged 25 to 54 (Gen X, Gen Y (millennials), and the older Gen Z), the majority are actually skeptical of the free market.

Perhaps this growing murmur of discontent with market function is why we're starting to hear more socialized talk these days, including the need for the government to step in and regulate our high drug prices. As noted, some legislators who favor drug cost regulation may not think of this as part of socialized medicine, but it is.

Much of the best past and current data about healthcare patterns and healthcare cost has come from studying Medicare data, whose results and outcomes are routinely reviewed. Medicare payments for many goods and services are often much lower than the inflated charges you are asked to pay if you're uninsured or privately insured; however, despite some disagreement, Medicare's lower payments are probably much closer to real cost.

Medicare is a government-regulated healthcare *insurance* system. It is better described as a socialized insurance system than socialized medicine. Most providers such as doctors who accept the insurance will not be government employees; we would be contractors of sorts. Most hospitals, labs, drug companies, and manufacturers will not be government-owned.

Most of the people who currently have Medicare are satisfied. It is not perfect – no system is – but in general we know Medicare is more focused on the health of patients and the health of our economy – it is not driven by profit. It is the government that has the most transparent view of healthcare. Our government has the legal right and obligation to penetrate the veil of secrecy.

It is true that the private sector also seeks to save costs, but to boost their bottom line and not because of concern for our economy or patients.

Medicare for All is too often dismissively

regarded by some as not realistic, because it will be too expensive. *Will it be too expensive?* is the wrong question. The better question is, *Does it have to be too expensive?* The answer is, *Absolutely not,* unless you have the preference, consciously or otherwise, to see it go bankrupt. Actually, the best question about Medicare for All would be, *Could it save money?* The answer is, *Absolutely yes.*

If other wealthy nations can figure out a way to provide healthcare that performs better at much lower cost to all of its citizens, why can't we? Canada and South Korea, who both have their own version of Medicare for All, spend a lot less than we do and perform better. Are we simply too stupid to figure out how to do it? Ridiculous!

That our American healthcare experiment to create a corporate-first, profit-driven private system instead of a patient-first, government-regulated system does not work well, should not lead to criticism of those who chose this direction many decades ago. As noted above, our capitalistic intentions were sensible and understandable. That many peer nations after World War II *all* happened to choose or continue government-run systems is more likely related to their healthcare histories and cultural philosophy than to any clairvoyance that the free market wouldn't work in healthcare.

Using our *Homo sapiens* gift of innovative creativity, is it possible that we are smart enough to gradually build a new Medicare system? Is it possible that we can provide universal coverage, save money for many if not most American families, save our economy a lot of money, and improve our healthcare performance? Why not? The idea that Medicare might actually save money is not just misrepresented, it is often absent from public discussion.

Every family is different. In Chapter 12, I shared Ronnie's and my personal story of the significant amount of money – *at least* $176,000 – that we've saved since being on Medicare. Only about 14 percent of Americans, those of us who before Medicare bought our own insurance in the private market, might have benefited as much as we did. But the perspective that Medicare cost is unsustainable is misinformation.

A much larger cohort of Americans who have employer-based insurance will likely feel comfortable with that private set up until they understand what they will get with Medicare. Allow me to stir that pot.

If Medicare becomes an option, your employer may have the right to choose and pay for Medicare for the entire company. In fact, if Medicare gains sway, employers who may no longer have to provide insurance, will probably have to contribute to our new Medicare finances, but not as much as they were paying in the private market, and with much less administrative hassle.

If you have employer-based insurance, it is occasionally changed abruptly and you have to swim in a new medical stream, often with different physicians. With straight Medicare, unless your physician moves, retires, or dies, you are very likely to be able to keep your doctor for the rest of your life. But if you want to change, you can. There are no restrictions like those imposed in the private market or with Medicare Advantage.

No one is excluded from Medicare because of pre-existing conditions. Thus, the factor that causes private insurance to raise prices when they have to accept patients with higher projected medical costs is already a nonfactor with Medicare.

Individual deductibles and copays with Medicare are generally lower compared to those of private policies. Also, there would be no annual or lifetime caps like those that exist with private policies. For these and other reasons, some argue that the out-of-pocket spending on healthcare for American patients, over a lifetime, will substantially *decrease* if we adopt Medicare for All. I'm in that camp.

The annual per capita cost for all healthcare in America has risen to over $11,000. Medicare currently provides healthcare to the sickest, most costly part of our population, seniors and disabled. Medicare is also responsible for paying the last few medical months of a long life. The cost of this end-of-life care is astronomical.

Despite the skew toward inflated expenses with the elderly, the overall per capita cost of caring for current Medicare patients is remarkably similar to that of the general population. Since Medicare has taken on our most unhealthy and expensive part of the patient spectrum, why isn't the Medicare per capita cost higher than the average per capita cost for the whole country? The answer seems obvious: Even with some legislative roadblocks, like not being able to negotiate with pharmaceutical companies to lower drug prices (and that can be fixed), Medicare already does a much better job at controlling costs than the private insurance industry.

Important to understand is that the youngest seniors eligible for Medicare at age 65 cost only about $5,000 per capita, less than one half the current national rate. If Medicare were covering everyone, including the vastly larger, younger than 65 portion of the population, it's not a big leap to imagine that our overall per capita cost for healthcare might be quite a bit lower.

Some pundits, and others who should know better, pontificate that the approximately $3.5 trillion currently spent annually on healthcare in the U.S. is so astronomical that the "added" burden of Medicare will be impossible to bear. Hogwash! The most likely possibility is a *reduced* burden for we patients, and for the American economy.

One of the future shock problems to be discussed in the next chapter is job loss, attributable in part to rapid societal change. We've seen this in mining and manufacturing. With the adoption of Medicare, many private insurance jobs will be lost. It is possible, however, that between private supplemental policies and Medicare Advantage, a substantial number of private insurance employees will be able to keep their jobs. In addition, some workers currently in the private sector could be absorbed in the government work force.

Inevitably, however, some jobs in the private insurance sector will go. For those individuals who do lose jobs, we must show appropriate respect for the dignity of their work. We need to honor what people have contributed to our society by providing necessary retraining and financial support during a transition. We need compassion.

Comedian Billy Crystal had a schtick on his TV show in which he played a security guard having an "I hate when that happens" conversation with a fellow guard:

So, one night these two guards were walking the halls of the building they were protecting, and Crystal says something like, "You know what I really hate?"

His buddy says, "What's that?"

"I hate when you take a vegetable peeler and jam it up your nose and take it and scrape it around the inside of your nose. I can't stand it. It hurts so bad."

His buddy says, "Oh yeah, I know exactly what you mean. I hate when that happens."

To me, especially in hindsight and with my experience in studying our healthcare situation, these conversations are reflective of our current partisan political environment in which logic is conspicuously absent. And in some respects, I have come to regard the private side of our healthcare system as that vegetable peeler, a self-inflicted, painful, not rational, unnecessary encumbrance.

My ideal healthcare system for America is one that would help patients and our economy through good times and bad by providing universal health insurance for life, as does every other wealthy nation on the planet. It would also be much less expensive.

In our Assholistic pre-Obamacare era, I described our private insurance environment as having six levels of coverage. Using the criteria of how well patients are covered by insurance, from worst to best they are: no insurance, putrid insurance, poor insurance, fair insurance, good insurance, and excellent insurance.

The Affordable Care Act was intended to eliminate or reduce the bottom end, the no-insurance category and the putrid category, which to some extent it did. Putrid policies were not allowed to be sold on the exchanges because they provided a sort of illusion that you had insurance, but the deductibles and copays were so high and with so many exclusions of coverage, that often the insured almost couldn't use the policy unless catastrophe struck. Remember, under the Trump administration, resumption of putrid policy sales was resurrected.

At the top end, only straight Medicare with good private supplemental policies, and some expensive private policies, ever made it to the excellent category.

According to T.R. Reid in *The Healing of America,* four basic systems of healthcare financing can be found in any and every country in the world. I would amend that to five:

1. The "Private" European Model

Islands of healthcare finance in the United States

may track the so-called private insurance model developed in Germany (championed by Chancellor Otto von Bismark in the late nineteenth century), but for the most part, this is very unlike our private system.

This is the system used by France, Japan, Germany, Belgium, and the Netherlands. Every one of these countries ranks higher than the United States in healthcare delivery.

On balance, these universal systems are patient-friendly and economy-friendly, but they in no way have any resemblance to a free market capitalistic operation. Unlike America, universal coverage is mandatory. This private insurance is not really private; it is almost entirely under the thumb of government. About a hundred different "private" nonprofit insurance companies, called "sickness funds," must pay the exact same amount for equivalent service.

The funding of this insurance is generally not tied to employment, but at times can be. The system is financed by progressive taxation. All funds go into a central pool and are distributed to the various sickness funds by the government.

Copays are also progressive. Up to a prescribed

limit, you pay more if you are wealthier. Profit for the insurance companies is *not* the goal; service to patients and economic efficiency for the country are the drivers.

Developed gradually over the past 150 years, this German-originated system does work well. It would probably be more difficult to implement in the United States where we already have Medicare, and we would still have real private insurance in the form of supplemental policies. As an abstraction, however, the European model does have merit.

2. Government Owned

The second healthcare financing strategy is the government-owned (not government-regulated) model, financed through taxes and developed in England in the twentieth century. Here the government is the primary payer with costs and services tightly controlled. This universal system is found in England, Italy, and Spain; their healthcare ranks higher than American healthcare and costs much less than our system. The government-owned model is represented in America through the Indian

Health Service, parts of the military services, and the Veterans Administration.

3. National Health Insurance

This is our Medicare and is the primary system found in Canada and South Korea. In our current Medicare environment, our government's Medicare costs are somewhat inflated because our current Medicare covers the sicker part of our population, the elderly and disabled, and also because Medicare is legislatively required to pay "market" high prices for some goods and services. The universal Medicare systems of Canada and South Korea rank higher than our current private-public hybrid, and again their per capita costs are lower.

4. Self-Pay

This is not the major model of any wealthy nation, but all nations have some healthcare that is paid for by direct exchange of money or barter for service. This model is less a system and more a default mode, especially in countries that have little healthcare available. In these countries, people are often without access to healthcare much of the time.

5. The American Hybrid Model

We are definitely in an era in which some people in the U.S. want to minimize any role that the government plays in the public-private dance. Government is taboo. The only game is or should be private. But in reality, two-thirds of all healthcare in the United States is already paid for with taxpayer dollars. The "socialized" horse is already out of the barn. With the possible exception of Canada and South Korea, our American model is the only one amongst our peers that significantly embraces this multifaceted private-public hybrid.

American healthcare already has at least six *government-managed* entities that are primarily socialized: Medicare, Medicaid, Children's Hospital Insurance Program (CHIP), prison healthcare, and Workers Compensation. In addition, we have two more primarily socialized *government-owned* healthcare systems: The Department of Veterans Affairs (VA) and the Indian Health Service. Then there is military medicine that in and of itself is a primarily socialized *mixture* of government-owned and government-managed care.

Despite our complicated hybrid system, or perhaps because of it, about one-third of American citizens are poorly insured or uninsured. Yet with one-third poorly insured, our per capita spending is still by far the highest in the world. To have approximately one-third of our population with no insurance, or putrid to poor insurance, does not save money. It drives patients to more expensive crisis care, with more continuing chronic illness.

My conclusion that Medicare would be our best approach was not clear to me when I began to explore our healthcare problems some years ago. It simply became apparent that unless we extracted our healthcare system from the jaws of healthcare's free market dysfunction and pulled the damn vegetable peeler out of our collective noses, we would continue to be losers both healthwise and financially.

Medicare will increasingly be in the news. There

will be a growing chorus of criticism from misinformed, ambivalent, or hostile special interest groups. Not too long ago, one of today's journalists for whom I have great respect wrote about this.

David Brooks (author of *The Second Mountain,* which I highly recommend) wrote an op-ed in *The New York Times* March 5, 2019, entitled *The Impossible 'Medicare for All.'* Discussion of two elements of his op-ed may serve to demonstrate how complex this subject is, and how easy it is to present possible misinformation or incomplete information without malice.

To fully appreciate hospital economics would require substantially more financial and accounting sophistication than I currently have. So, to explore these issues, I sought the counsel of a friend, David Deprin; we began our conversations a few years ago, long before the op-ed. Warning: there are some twists and turns in this tale of economic complexity, so if you become bored, just skip it.

David has been a longtime senior financial officer of hospitals and major health systems. His next to last professional incarnation was as the CFO of a large hospital in Texas. And then for seven years before his recent retirement, he was director of accounting locally for Ascension, the largest not-for-profit hospital system in the U.S., which has three of their hospitals in my area.

Ascension is one of four multi-hospital systems in Jacksonville. One of those other systems, also not-for-profit (and the system that recruited me to Florida from Vermont almost thirty years ago), now reportedly has the equivalent of a billion dollar endowment. This reflects the accumulation of income from its four local not-for-profit hospitals, as well as income from various outpatient entities such as physician groups and outpatient diagnostic centers owned by the hospitals' for-profit subsidiaries. All such funding is segregated into very special legal silos with great care by compliance officers who are often attorneys. Everything is hopefully scrupulously legal.

Given the complexity of the topic and the idiosyncrasy of different hospital systems, my goal with David's help was to simply create an impressionist canvas of hospital finance, rather than a 20-megapixel digital photograph.

David Brooks reported that Medicare underpays hospitals: "Medicare reimburses hospitals at 87 percent of costs while private insurance reimburses at 145 percent of costs." If that entirely represents the story, why then do hospitals in which the substantial majority of the patient population is insured by Medicare not only survive but, according to my David, often do quite well?

First, Medicare has more transparency related to actual hospital expense. It reportedly tries to set reimbursements that are adequate to cover real costs but leave some profit. Overall the average hospital expects to collect about 35 percent (or a little more) of the amount they bill from a diverse patient population. If a hospital is filled with only Medicare (and Medicaid) patients, 100 percent pay. Usually, however, hospitals have the complex task of figuring out how to best account for income from Medicare (and Medicaid), all the while taking into account the amount of billing that is not paid by private insurance or self-pay. (That non-pay amount may be different than non-billed pro-bono work.)

Second, hospitals do not practice accounting

shyness related to their estimated financial needs. They independently define what *they* consider to be the amount necessary to get by, an amount almost always higher than the Medicare estimate. If the hospital is somehow overpaid by Medicare, it must return money; thus, it is to the hospital's advantage to realistically legally project Medicare underpayment.

Inputting all the variables, the hospital accountants, actuaries, and perhaps IBM's Watson must figure out how to achieve the hospital's financial goals and make it all work. To project a lower percentage Medicare reimbursement, and to account for all of the private insurance, no-insurance, under payment and non-payment, hospitals impose inflated charges across the board. Once programmed, the hospital's chargemaster produces bills that at times reach ludicrous levels, sometimes 100 times cost, like a 1.5 cent Tylenol tablet for $1.50, as noted in the amazing 2013 *TIME* article by Steven Brill, "Bitter Pill: Why Medical Bills Are Killing Us."

Third, and important but not widely known, when the hospital reports underpayment by Medicare, in some circumstances the government *reimburses* the hospital for the shortfall.

Fourth, prices allowed for hospital outpatient services are often above and beyond what nonhospital outpatient services can charge. This sort of outpatient profit shifting may, to different degrees, make up for inpatient shortfalls, but wouldn't be part of the hospital reimbursement picture.

The point is that hospital finances are complicated and even apparently simple direct statistics, like "Medicare reimburses hospitals at 87 percent of costs" can be officially correct, yet inadequately convey the moving parts of the full picture.

The other issue from Mr. Brooks's op-ed that I referred to above is the larger concern that Medicare would be a financial drain on the economy. How would we assess this? A rising per capita cost would suggest a financial drain on the American economy. A diminished per capita cost would suggest a "refund" to America, and to patients as individuals.

Based upon information from the Mercatus Center at George Mason University, Mr. Brooks reported the following: "The Sanders plan would raise federal spending by about $32.6 trillion over its first 10 years."

At the current time, our healthcare is costing more than $3.5 trillion a year. Over the next ten years, with inflation and without any change to our current system, the cost of healthcare would already be at least $35 trillion. *And there would be an additional $32.6 trillion on top of that?*

Whether or not the Mercatus information is accurate, there are blueprints for implementing Medicare other than Senator Sanders's program. But more to the point, how do we square this Mercatus information with the November 2018 *Economic Analysis of Medicare for All* produced by The Political Economy Research Institute of the University of Massachusetts Amherst?

> "Medicare for All has the potential to achieve major cost savings in its operations relative to the existing U.S. healthcare system. We estimate through implementation of Medicare for All that overall U.S. healthcare costs would fall by about 19 percent relative to the existing system. The most significant sources of cost saving will be in three areas: 1) administration – 9 percent savings in

total system costs; 2) pharmaceutical pricing – 5.9 percent savings in system costs; and 3) establishing uniform Medicare rates for hospitals, physicians and clinics – 2.8 percent savings in system costs."

That is almost 19 percent savings of our current annual $3.5 trillion-dollar healthcare cost – that's huge! Special interests definitely don't want Medicare to become the single-payer system in America; they do not want to see their unfair Magic Kingdom of super profit disappear. They understandably may promote negative projections of the overall economic impact of Medicare. I cannot say this too often: with our flawed healthcare free market, I believe it is far more likely that per capita cost would rise with the continuation of the for-profit Obamacare/private insurance model but could actually fall with not-for-profit Medicare.

On March 6, 2019, Canadian physician Amy Fraser responded to the op-ed:

"David Brooks suggests that the transition to single-payer health insurance would be too disruptive for America to tolerate. Doctors like their income, insurance workers like their jobs and (most) Americans like their insurance, after all. I'm not sure, however, why disruption is often considered permissible when done by innovators for profit, and intrusive and feckless when done by governments to save lives.

As a physician working in the Canadian system, I can't pretend that universal insurance is without its flaws. It's true that the implementation of our version of "Medicare for All" took decades and involved plenty of disarray, including doctors' strikes. We have fraud and waste, just as you do – but we also have healthier people for a fraction of the cost. Implement universal Medicare already, if only to stop the moralizing from north of the border."

Changing how we think about healthcare, eliminating our profit-first philosophy and replacing it with a kinder patient-first coherent system like Medicare may be difficult, but that should not deter us from trying. We must continue our quest to serve all patients as well as we can – that's what healthcare,

Hippocrates, and compassion are all about.

As we struggled through the Great Recession beginning in 2008, I thought about the reduction in stress we would have felt if we all had affordable healthcare such as Medicare, independent of job or even whether we were working. Then I began to speculate about market forces. Interestingly, with both the healthcare and the housing bubble, the actual market problems were similar – a working gas pedal as cost accelerator, but no good braking system to provide restraint. In provoking our 2008 recession, the housing market temporarily developed "brake failure." Loans were granted too easily. Prices rose but the brakes were broken because of human tinkering and greed motivated dishonesty. We managed to bandage that situation with modest regulation of the dishonesty; but bandages are only temporary.

What the Great Recession really suggested to me, however, was the powerful influence of future shock (see next chapter). Human nature has been around for a long time; the intense technology allowing manic manipulation of our economy has not. Those that wield the levers have never had such power. And, as a result, the current degree of financial inequality in America is astonishing.

To some degree the old United States of America is fading, but hidden in plain sight is a new nation: The United Banks and Corporations of America, with racial inequality and economic injustice for mostly all. Disparate healthcare is a foundational factor in the inequities equation.

We need a broader understanding of our problems and a new progressive approach to a market truly aligned with quality of life for the vast majority of Americans, especially Americans of color. Nothing less will do. How ironic that we're just now (maybe) beginning to understand the unrelenting racial prejudice that we've inflicted on people of color in this nation. Slavery was a fiscal policy; slaves were regarded as a commodity, providing the fiscal engine that was substantially responsible for launching this nation on a trajectory of economic greatness. No wonder there's so much anger.

Is recovery possible? I don't know. But the power and speed of future shock can work just as well for right thinking as wrong thinking. (Again, what is future shock? I'm getting there.)

We need new economics, where wealth relates to life, liberty, and happiness for all. Let's begin by turning away from a healthcare system that has cloaked America in healthcare mediocrity and unevenness. Let's embrace a healthcare system that is more compassionate and puts the best interests of patients and the economy ahead of the financial health of corporations.

Medicare makes American healthcare compassionate – for all. Let's start there, and perhaps other change will follow.

Part III
Future Shock and Beyond

The saddest aspect of life right now is that science gathers knowledge faster than society gathers wisdom.

– *Isaac Asimov*

Chapter 16
Future Shock Meets America

Writing *Patients Before Profits* has been a labor of love, filled with personal excitement. Exploring ideas and expanding my world vision is a joy. I'm not upset by understanding how little I know compared to what might eventually be known. And I'm still as excited about learning, maybe even more than I was in my youth, during a time when I understood less about life.

After more than a dozen years of exploring and

writing about healthcare policy, economics, and the importance of compassion and kindness, this "autumn" project, *Patients Before Profits,* is about to be published.

Whatever you think about the book, it comes from the heart and is not intended to be political. I have never been much of an activist. I don't feel connected to the politics of parties. Since I first voted when I was eighteen, I have registered NPA, no party affiliation. A number of months ago, however, I was one of eight physicians who authored and circulated a letter to Jacksonville's mayor, pleading from a medical position that he impose CDC health restrictions on the Republican National Convention scheduled to take place in Jacksonville. We signed that letter on a Friday. Somehow, over that weekend, the letter exploded into view, garnering the public support of more than five hundred local physicians.

We were contacted by a group of prominent attorneys who were working pro bono representing residents of Jacksonville living near the convention facilities with the same goals in mind. Between us, them, and other influences, the Republican National Convention never came to Jacksonville.

Our group of eight continued to talk is now called Doctors Fighting COVID. Given our medical backgrounds and knowledge, we try to comment to the public and to politicians how we *feel* about various health strategies related to COVID. We share how we feel personally about the conduct of public health in Florida. As we work with other physician groups, we try not to pontificate or politicize.

As a psychiatrist, I believe that emotion, often not logical, frequently drives policy and politics more than evidence and facts. We are experiencing a time in America that will be regarded as historically epic, a time when emotion seems to have especially held sway.

Although Doctors Fighting COVID often disagrees with what we believe to be medically inappropriate public and political sentiment, we respect the absolute right of anyone to honestly share whatever *feelings* they have. It matters that you are honest about those feelings; then you are telling your truth. So, I'm going to share my truth.

I'm not an angry person, but when I encounter someone in my environment these days who is not wearing a mask, I feel assaulted. And that induces fear, anger, sadness, and a feeling of being disrespected.

Doctors Fighting COVID does its best to approach such personal truth as sacrosanct, for both us and those who may not agree with us. If we simply report how we feel when others disregard what may be lifesaving medical guidelines, our feelings are real. And the feelings of others who disagree with us are also real, no matter how incorrect we believe they are. Hopefully, by taking this sort of respectful approach, we can better listen to one another. However, what is most important is not what you say to someone, it's what they hear. So, I expect that some of you may, nonetheless, "hear" what I'm about to say as partisan and political – that is not the intent.

According to a Jeffrey Toobin *The New Yorker* article (Dec. 24 & 31, 2018), an unlikely dinner grouping occurred a few years back that included Senator John McCain, Congressman Adam Schiff, the singer Bono, and Bill Gates. Following one of many shared jokes, possibly one about being of Irish descent, Bono said, "You know I love Ireland, I'm a proud Irishman. Ireland is a great country, but it's not an idea. America is not just a country; it's an idea."

What makes America an idea? What distinguishes America as different, or special? It is not our high per capita income. It is not because of our abundant natural resources, our national parks, or geographical area. These are contributing factors but not explanatory.

The exceptional gift of our Founding Fathers was their attempt to create a system of governance that embraced the beauty and creative diversity of human uniqueness. With a philosophical stance reflected in the Declaration of Independence and the Constitution, they fostered a special niche for America.

We are a nation of difference, not sameness. Our forebears embraced a kind of humanitarian integrity, placing value in fairness and equality of the human spirit. This mix is our power, our beauty, our hybrid vigor, but also our nemesis. There were big problems from the beginning. Because of the blind spots of society at the time of the American Revolution, although the founders espoused equality between all "men," this lofty aspiration actually did not include women, Indians, and most of all slaves. It took a few hundred years to begin to make amends, and we're still struggling with our melting pot. Where we are in this journey toward humanitarian dignity is a matter of debate. I see progress, but we have a way to go.

I've long considered the word "idiosyncrasy" to be a guiding light when I treat patients. I see every human being as unique. I don't generalize and assume that you and the next patient will react the same way to the same medication, and so it goes.

No two people on this planet, whether or not of similar race, are exactly the same. Part of our differences reflect experience. For instance, the most profound educational experience for most human beings is during the first five or six years of life. That is when we are enrolled in Childhood University, where parents or other family members are the professors. Interestingly, however, the way each of us experiences our experiences is biologically modified by our unique brains and life machines (bodies), blueprinted for that uniqueness by our genes.

Country, city of origin, racial and religious influences, behaviors of our family, experience with peers and such all play a part. While these different experiences are important, each one is filtered and modified for that uniqueness by our genetics.

There used to be a number of human species on earth, and now there's just one; every person on earth is part of the *Homo sapiens* gang. Therefore, every human genetic blueprint is dramatically similar; however, the miniscule genetic differences between individuals that do exist are profoundly influential in our uniqueness.

Color of skin plays a continuing political role in our societal struggles, but only a minor scientific role in the genetic spectrum of human difference. I'm reminded of the old cliché: you can't judge a book by its cover. But far too many of us do. Many of us of different skin color have a lot in common; many who have similar skin color are very different.

Racially, the Civil War was a specific turning point, but the war is not over. Racial prejudice had perhaps moderated a bit over time, but recently our culture seems more fractured.

As I reflect on the major influences driving partisanship during this historical time, the browning of society is probably of increasing significance. The rapidly approaching time when white Americans will be in the minority is consciously or subconsciously disturbing to a lot of people. There are many who are suggesting this. Whether true or not, what is very clear is that differences of all types have been increasingly disrespected. Contentiousness and conflict are pervasive; anger and incivility are palpable. Our partisan divide continues to deepen.

Although some politicians who currently or recently had leadership positions in American society have warts, it is far more likely that preeminence of weak or challenged leaders is more a symptom of our problems than a cause. Why has that happened? Why do so many of us realistically feel left behind? Why do so many of us feel as though we're getting a raw deal in life? Why is the dream of American exceptionalism, democracy, and humanitarian equality being challenged?

Browning is a partial answer, but there is at least one other particular problem that I believe is a major contributor to our tumult, yet infrequently receives mention, and is little understood. I'll name it the "*acceleration pandemic.*"

Life has many memorable pivotal moments. Life-altering moments may be times of great beauty, emotion, or insight. When I was twenty-eight, I read a book that changed the way I looked at the world.

To this day, Alvin Toffler's *Future Shock*, published in 1970, influences my perspective. This is the opening sentence of the book: "In the three short decades between now and the twenty-first century, millions of ordinary, psychologically ordinary people, will face a collision with the future."

Toffler opined that the availability of information and technology was expanding so rapidly that human beings would have to adapt dramatically in order to understand and live effectively in the future – which is now. Thomas Friedman's book *Thank You for Being Late* confirms and expands Toffler's insight.

Modern humans (approximately the past ten thousand years) have adapted to change faster than any other species, but we're now on a new playing field that raises the ante. Toffler's prediction was indeed prescient. We are perhaps experiencing a singular moment in the limited history of humankind, one that is potentially both painful and amazing. Suddenly, in the proverbial blink of an historical eye, as recognized by Toffler, an unprecedented explosion of technology and information accelerated to warp speed, testing human adaptive capacity. In the past, more than any other animal species, humans have had to adapt to rapid change, but nothing like now. Human resilience is being stress tested. Few if any of our ancestors ever came close to experiencing the speed of change that's occurring now. It's as though we've awakened and found ourselves on some sort of alien planet.

Perhaps our recent decades of growing societal divisiveness and our two world wars demonstrate the stress predicted by Toffler. There are those who might disagree and consider our growing antisocial trends, our political partisanship, and racial prejudice to be business as usual and who will say *it's always been this way.* I doubt it.

I believe the current level of increasing pressure to adapt more rapidly in the face of the unrelenting acceleration of technology is a new challenge, especially considering the unprecedented access to partisan silos of information and misinformation. "People-quakes" (seemingly seismic social fractures) and intransigent partisanship will become worse unless we are meaningfully resilient and able to resolve our issues, not just like we have in the past, but better than before.

In healthcare, and I suspect in other disciplines, there is a growing need to abandon creaking and dysfunctional approaches to problem solving that no longer work. If we can't, as my then three-year-old cousin astutely said to her grandmother many years ago, "I'm in deep shit aren't I, Grandma?"

The problems of our accelerating world are on display as we watch cultural norms crack. Vocational discombobulation is rampant because of the sudden expansion of technology; jobs disappear, whole segments of industrial work painfully vanishes, and armed conflict increasingly employs cyber bullets rather than lead bullets.

Much of the challenge we face is not entirely conscious. The impact of our warp-speed world to some degree provokes deeper levels of thought, what Daniel Kahneman refers to in *Thinking Fast and Slow* as the fast thinking subconscious, rather than our slower conscious awareness. Some of us feel demeaned. We harden philosophical and political positions. Amplified prejudice, partisanship, and anger become symptoms of our subconscious struggle. In the face of our semi-invisible struggle to manage this overload, we are drawn to emotional positions of security where life feels simpler again.

I don't yet know how we'll cope. We enjoy both privilege and challenge because of this unprecedented acceleration. Society can break apart, or we can adapt and take advantage of innovation and abundance that has not before been available.

Looking back, although it was not apparent, modern man began to board this rocket ship about five hundred years ago (see *Sapiens* by Uval Noah Harari). For a while, however, after "liftoff," the acceleration was slow, barely noticeable. As we now continue into "deep space," those of us more recently onboard – perhaps those of us specifically born between the late nineteenth and very early twenty-first centuries – bear the brunt of this unprecedented challenge. The acceleration has become exponential. I'll use my life as an example.

At the time of my toddlerhood, mid-twentieth century, the development of the next generation was expected to take about fifteen to twenty years. Now, generational change may have shrunk to four or five years.

When I was a small boy, I remember visiting Dock Street in Philadelphia with my father and watching horses (not just trucks) pulling produce carts over cobblestones; I remember that no homes had television.

At the University of Pennsylvania, not far from cobblestoned Dock Street, as I turned three, the thirty-ton Eniac computer was being fired up for the first time. Still, I completed college, medical school, law school, a medical internship, and a psychiatric residency – *all without a computer.* I now carry a phone in my pocket weighing ounces that is dramatically more powerful than the thirty-ton behemoth at Penn, and more powerful than most of the computers I've used since the early eighties.

It was a short thirty-nine years before my birth that Wilbur and Orville Wright flew at Kittyhawk. I was twenty-six years old when Neil Armstrong walked on the moon, and fifty-five years old when the Rover landed on Mars.

In 1943, I was but five months old when Albert Hoffman, a chemist with Sandoz Pharmaceutical in Switzerland, was inadvertently exposed to a tiny quantity of LSD 25, a compound he had invented five years earlier that initially seemed to have little medical use. This accidental exposure triggered an experience that Hoffman considered dramatic and mind-expanding. He had scientifically synthesized a class of drugs that were eventually labeled "psychedelics."

These new drugs are not really new at all; they are related to chemicals that were already existing in nature and used for eons by different cultures. But Hoffman's discovery opened a modern portal. LSD was at first greeted with enthusiasm by some in the scientific and medical communities. Then, about twenty years after their discovery, psychedelics went dark for a number of reasons. They were legally ostracized, and most research was discontinued.

That was the situation when I began my psychiatric residency in 1975. However, Michael Pollan's recent book *How to Change Your Mind* explains why Albert Hoffman and other early researchers' original instincts about the potential therapeutic utility of psychedelics may have been correct in the first place. Important new research will be emerging.

Even without considering direct patient treatment, during the era of my training, these new molecules provoked a bevy of other basic research in neuroscience resulting in new conceptions of brain function, some related to the now well-known neurotransmitter serotonin.

A new era in psychiatry was born, but it took a few years for the emerging neuroscience momentum to become integrated into the training of young physicians. My residency experience was distinctly lacking in neuroscience compared to those residents who began their journey just five years after I did. As a mostly pre-neuroscience-trained psychiatrist, I had to leap onto the psychiatry rocket and adapt to the explosion of brain knowledge as I went. It was a challenge but rewarding, intellectually stimulating, and beneficial to patients.

Moving on, in 1945 and shortly before my third birthday, an unrelated gargantuan double-edged sword of acceleration exploded onto the scene at Hiroshima and Nagasaki. When this happened, the world changed instantly.

And last but not least by a long shot, I believe

climate change is a direct consequence of many aspects of our acceleration. Inventions of petroleum-dependent machines yielded increasingly obese productions of carbon dioxide.

When I was born, there was little understanding of climate change. I was seven years old when a few scientists began to question the possibility of a trend. It took time, but it turned out they were onto something. Other than obvious change in fire, hurricane, and temperature patterns, shifts in disease patterns are also occurring. Different climate ecology leads to changing evolution of microorganisms, maybe including COVID. If we don't solve climate dysregulation, little else may matter.

I'm not certain where we are now, in part because if you try to pinpoint something, it's such a fast-moving target that it morphs almost instantly in front of our eyes. We've recently had a very contentious election. The pre- and post-election seismic people quakes, the partisan fervor, and societal venom we're experiencing, maybe even the attack on democracy and the American dream, are related to and facilitated by the onslaught of the future shock technology and information overload that Alvin Toffler predicted fifty years ago. Communication waterfalls like Fox News, CNN, MSNBC, News Max, Facebook, Twitter, Instagram and the like are, in my opinion, all part of that overload.

By way of contrast, think for a moment about the American Revolution. We have just celebrated the 247th anniversary (December 16, 1773) of the Boston Tea Party. If we had then, anything then like todays ability to communicate, King George would have had crucial military information instantly and it is quite possible that the United States of America would not exist.

My speculations notwithstanding, too many of us have little appreciation for the power of this new reality. The importance of societal acceleration seems somewhat muted, almost hidden as a concept amidst the raucous and near-continuous "breaking news" of the current twenty-four-hour cycle, the availability of Google, the changes in manufacturing, and people-quakes – rocket constructs all. To have any pretentions of preserving and improving future American specialness, we will require accelerating adaptive abilities.

So far, we may have made only modest accommodation to our rocket. In the past we were able to take societal breaths and get used to change. No more. We are now continuously in the throes of speeding up, of accelerating. *Always faster* is our new reality.

My grandchildren to whom this book is dedicated (and all future generations) will experience continuous acceleration as their normal. Because of new brain science, including neuroplasticity and epigenetic modification, there is some speculation that Lev and Ani's brains will wire differently than mine or even their parents. It remains to be seen whether this new normal will make adaptation easier for the new generations who know nothing else – time will tell. There is little doubt, however, that prodigious change will continue to impact broad aspects of modern life. Many of us would like this rocket to slow down, but it has launched; there's no turning back. Many of us may feel anxious and a bit out of control without knowing why. It is understandable that we might yearn for the sepia tones of the good old days, the comfort of the familiar simplicity of a bygone slower era that seems missing. Well, it ain't gonna happen.

If we are able to adapt, we might find ourselves in a landscape of resurgent vitality. If we cannot adapt, escalating chaos is likely to be the result. As an inveterate optimist, accepting the reality of that possible chaos is alien to my usual perspective, but I am profoundly concerned. We might just crash. I'm not at all sure what that would look like, but I do not want to find out.

I want to believe that we can adjust, but we can definitely mess it up. I'm saying that old ways of doing business will no longer work. It's like the familiar quote attributed to Einstein: *Insanity is continuing to do things the same way and expecting different results.* During the final few years of writing this book and developing The Patients Party, I've especially struggled to understand how we might approach this mess. How might we hack humanity for the better? As a psychiatrist, I tried to look at our dilemma from high above the clouds, both the atmospheric and computer-based kind. I found myself speculating that we might be able to learn not to react to disagreement with conflict and confrontation, and instead learn to react with kindness and compassion. This is the kind of hack we need.

Linking the health and compassion was unplanned when I began writing, but it has been a fortunate collaboration. I believe that health as a human value is so intrinsically meaningful, so necessary to all human beings, that it may have enough gravitas to provide the best soil for the tree of compassion to put down roots. For patients to increasingly react to all life with kindness and compassion is likely to improve health, and most other aspects of life. Maybe, just maybe, my initial focus on health that I began with years ago might allow some of us to retrain to compassion, rather than conflict and defense of our turf. Maybe we can break old habits, learn to react differently, think more for ourselves, uncouple from screeching TV stations, and forge new ways of decision-making that are more compassion-driven and less skewed or skewered by politics, money, and power.

In healthcare or any other aspect of our culture, we need to be resilient and, if possible, cultivate the technologic and informational benefits never before available. It would be wonderful if we could transform our social mess and make lemonade from lemons. It would be especially gratifying if we could begin to use our new technology and informational abundance in a way that honors the spirit of compassion and human uniqueness that was the conceptual dream of our Founding Fathers, even if they couldn't pull it off.

Far less elegant than Martin Luther King's dream, maybe even close to delusional, I too have a dream: making society kind and compassionate rather than conflicted and confrontational. I was heartened while listening to Thomas Friedman's *Thank You for Being Late.* I heard, "I repeat: Naivete is the new realism – naïve is thinking that we are going to survive as a species in the age of accelerations without learning to govern our new realms in new ways and our old realms in new ways. And yes, this is going to require some very rapid moral and social evolution."

So maybe my dream isn't crazy after all.

Recently, as we have been suffering through the coronavirus pandemic, Tom Friedman has been commenting on three other pandemics to which we've been exposed in the last twenty years; first, the terror pandemic of 9/11; next, the economic pandemic of 2008; then, and ongoing, the climate pandemic. In this chapter, I mentioned a fourth – the acceleration pandemic.

As you read further and learn about The Patients Party, our mission is to foster a contemporary fifth pandemic, a positive pandemic of health and compassion. The books of Peter Diamandis and Steven Kotler, especially their 2012 book *Abundance,* explain that what I'm describing as positive pandemics may also be spawned by the engine of acceleration.

Logic and reason are crucial attributes of society. However, as I often told patients, "If logic always determined how we do things, I'd be out of business." That might be true enough, but it's not an either-or situation. Without question, however, whether conscious or not, our emotional aquifer is a major driver of our personal poems.

Social and emotional adaptation to acceleration and the browning of America has been and will continue to be a Mount Everest-sized challenge. I'm yearning to say, "we can do it," but I'm not sure.

Future shock is here. This is the future.

You may think I'm small, but I have a universe inside my mind.

– Yoko Ono

Chapter 17
The Patients Party

Without health, many aspects of life are diminished. Unfortunately, our healthcare system is particularly confusing, shrouded in mystery by a fog of misinformation and ridiculous complexity. We want to change that, so we developed The Patients Party. We are a 501(c)(3) nonprofit, based in Vermont, dedicated to improving the well-being and quality of life of all Americans. The best of American healthcare is possibly the best in the world, but as a whole system, we are actually mediocre.

The Patients Party mission is: *To give patients a voice in the healing of healthcare and America.* We want America to put patients before profits. We want America to establish universal life-long healthcare that is realistic, excellent, protects patients financially, and saves patients money. And, of utmost importance, we hope that healthcare and society become more compassionate.

The original sin of American healthcare was the decision after World War II to allow profits instead of the best interests of patients to drive the system. This inflates costs. Corporations and others have treated the healthcare environment as a remarkable profit machine. It is no accident that our healthcare costs are by far the highest in the world, while our performance is consistently ranked as the worst of our thirty-some peer nations where patients' interest do come before money.

Correcting our deficiencies is possible and creating universal coverage is possible. These improvements can be accomplished while costs for you and our economy are reduced. Though we know that's not what you have been led to believe. We wondered: "What would happen if we had a dialog in which we educated patients, and in turn patients, educated us? Might this lead to new understanding and better solutions?" We believe that would be the case.

Work with us. We will try our best to remove the mystery. We believe your input will improve the system that is developed. Most of all, we believe you deserve to stand up for your values and interests, to become an agent of change contributing to the well-being, happiness, and quality of life for you, your family, and humanity. This is a movement, not a moment.

Whatever the outcome, patients deserve to have a place at the table and a voice in the process. That's what The Patients Party is about.

Please visit us at **www.patientsparty.org.**

Epilogue

A few years ago, three titans of industry, Jeff Bezos (Amazon), Warren Buffet (Berkshire Hathaway), and Jamie Dimon (JP Morgan Chase) formed a joint venture they named "Haven." The purpose of this effort was to find healthcare solutions in the private sector that addressed easier access to primary care, simplified insurance benefits, and lowered drug prices. They decided to close the company without achieving success. There are speculations as to why this didn't work that are probably best summarized by the well-known pundit

Donald Trump who said: "Who knew this healthcare stuff was so complicated?"

No kidding! Perhaps there is something about developing a universal healthcare system that government and the private sector can do together.

In *Patients Before Profits,* I've tried to address healthcare as well as quality of life. Stimulated by Bono's comment that America was not just a country but an idea as well, I was especially focused on current America fractures that contrasted with the ideas of our founders.

My father had a great interest in history – me, not so much until I began to write this book. The final book I read before putting down my pen (computer) was *First Principles: What America's Founders Learned from the Greeks and Romans and How That Shaped Our Country.* At the conclusion of his writing, esteemed author Thomas E. Ricks had ten suggestions about healing America. Taking the liberty of changing the order, putting first those suggestions that were most embraced by this book, and (parenthetically) commenting on his suggestions, here is his list:

1. Refocus on the public good (not money)
2. Promote, cultivate, and reward virtue in public life – but don't count on it
3. Rehabilitate "happiness" (but it's not just pleasure)
4. Wake up Congress
5. Respect our core institutions – and push them
6. Enrich the political vocabulary (like more words for socialism)
7. Reclaim the definition of "un-American"
8. Don't panic (be present and take the long view)
9. Curtail campaign finance (corporations are not people)
10. Know your history

Digital Index

All sales of this book support The Patients Party, and we are truly appreciative. At this moment it is a good bet that you are either holding the paper version in your hand, holding a kindle device, or listening on headphones or speakers. While we're not trying to prevent sales in any way, we decided to also make the book available on our website *without cost.* We are hoping to convey our sincere desire to expand understanding related to the importance of compassion and kindness, while at the same time expanding understanding about improving our healthcare system.

Readers of any version of *Patients Before Profits* can take advantage of digital technology by searching all content (words, phrases, dates, etc.) by downloading the free searchable copy of this book from our website (www.patientsparty.org) or also search directly when reading the Kindle edition of the book.

Also, on the website regardless of where you read *Patients Before Profits,* you will have the opportunity to submit book related questions and comments.

Acknowledgments

I am deeply indebted to my family. I honor the memory of my parents, Belle and Sam Burak.

Both of my parents were children of immigrants and grew up in very modest circumstances. My mother had four siblings, my father five, although one of his sisters died of diphtheria as a young child. I was very lucky; they provided me with wonderful opportunities, and each in their own way nourished my soul.

Belle Keiner Burak was a talented secret poet. Her words were often sad, belying her charm and wit. An outstanding student, she was diagnosed with tuberculosis during her first year of college and following her lengthy recovery, never resumed her education. She sublimated her disappointment by being a cheerleader for the education of her children. She departed from my life when she was eighty-six, a few years before I began working on this book. I am absolutely certain that in her family genome, there are a few snippets of DNA that force people to put words to paper.

J. Samuel Burak was a gentle, incisively intelligent man with warmth, dry humor, and most of all – humility. My birth in 1942 *during* World War II (pre-Baby Boomer) was the result of his having been ineligible to serve in the army. He had been struck by a truck in his 20s, fracturing his left knee and prematurely triggering severe arthritis. As a talented student and good athlete before his injury, he finished high school two years early at age sixteen and worked full time in a supermarket to pay for college while earning an accounting degree.

He began working in the food industry for a family well known in Philadelphia because they owned a famous restaurant called Bookbinders. He taught himself appropriate law and engineering, becoming skilled in a niche profession related to spoilage of food during transportation. He eventually started his own business. He was a man of absolute integrity who instilled trust in those who worked with him. By the age of thirty-seven he was able to hire an architect and build a lovely home in a Philadelphia suburb called Elkins Park. I was seven when we moved in.

He was fifty-four when he suffered his first heart attack. I was in medical school in Philadelphia and was living on campus. I moved home to spend more time with him, staying overnight whenever I wasn't on call. Despite having had a warm and loving relationship growing up, those few years together were important. I had just begun to know him as an adult when he died at fifty-seven; I was twenty-six at the time, living on the Navajo Reservation in Arizona. His passing left a profound hole in my life.

Ronnie, my partner and love of my life has been my strongest supporter, my most astute critic, and my constant friend. Each time I would tell her, "I've really finished the book this time," she just smiled.

Julia and Eli Burakian, my daughter-in-law and son, the parents of Levon Sage Burakian and Ani Blaze

Burakian (to whom this book is dedicated), have my love and respect. They are wonderful together, great parents, and quietly bestow on my life a consistent feeling of happiness that sustains me.

My sister, Connie Rubinstein, a far better writer than I, has provided loving support and editorial expertise and I am grateful. I miss her husband, Robert Rubinstein, and honor his memory. His collection of edgy jokes has never been approached by anyone else I've ever known.

Johanna Bates, Connie's daughter (also better at words than her uncle), her husband, Colin Mitchell, and their son Emlyn add much to my happiness; I see them all too infrequently.

I honor the memory of Johanna's father, George Bates, a sweet, unforgettable, brilliant man whose passing made me sad.

Shirley Shils, my wonderful mother–in-law, was still living at home when she sadly passed away at age one hundred about a month before the publication of this book. Hers was a truly remarkable life. She raised three accomplished children, was an active leader in Jewish philanthropy, always supported her professor husband, started college at Penn at age fifty-five, earned her undergraduate degree at seventy and her Master's in Social Gerontology at seventy-five, and supported her family and friends with continuous love, grace, and gravitas. I am deeply appreciative of the love and support she showed me, our son Eli, his wife Julia, and their children Lev and Ani to whom this book is dedicated. I'm especially thankful that she was Ronnie's mother. Her love was totally reciprocated. My relationship with Shirley bore no resemblance to any mother-in-law joke you've ever heard.

When my father passed away, Ronnie's dad, Ed Shils, was always there for me and did all he could to support me above and beyond a typical father-in-law role. Ed passed away at age eighty-nine, still teaching at the Wharton School of the University of Pennsylvania. He enjoyed an exceptional life and career as he combined a loving nature and unusual intellect with grace.

Nancy Shils and Barry Shils have become sister and brother, not sister-in-law and brother-in-law. Both have actively supported my efforts in producing this book. Barry and I have especially enjoyed a sharing of support; his profession as a filmmaker has included not only producing but writing and directing. Sometimes we do a bit of brainstorming.

Nancy's son Max Szczurek is not just a nephew, he's a friend. He is my favorite nephew by far, and although he is my only nephew, if there were more he would still be my favorite. Just as Max is six months younger than Eli, his daughter Ariana is six months younger than my grandson Levon, and his son Eduardo is about six months younger than my granddaughter Ani.

Deborrah Hoag, my editor, is extraordinary – a dynamic, multi-talented eclectic writer and center of energy. I asked that she "sandpaper" this book, not only to eliminate mistakes, but to add insight and soul; she's done that and more. She will continue to add value to our website and The Patients Party in general as we evolve. Her work provides me with great comfort.

When a book is in process over a twelve-year period, many people help in many ways; I began to think about all of the people who have impacted my journey during these years and even before. The following lengthy list reflects uncertainty that I'll write another book or have another context in which to publicly acknowledge many people who I so appreciate. There are probably a few individuals not listed who I will recall after the book is in print. I will feel chagrined.

In mostly alphabetical order my thanks go to the following people: Kinney Adams; Margo Adams; Yvette Hyter-Adams; Bernie Alberda; Verna Alberda; Tom Alkoff; Dave Anderson; Molly Anderson; Syed Asad; David Belkin; Alisha Ben-Hamo; John Bennet; Noel Bennet; Laura Benson; Deddy Ben-Yaacov; Elizabeth Ben-Yaacov; Maia Ben-Yaacov; Shai Ben-Yaacov (and his lovely wife Kate Dugan); Gil Ben-Yaacov; Amos Ben-Yaacov; Tal Ben-Yaacov (and his recent bride Priyanka Nalamada): Susan Berard; Steven Biel; Harper Biel; David Blackmon; Steven Blitch; Stella Bryskin; Karen Campbell; Gabriella Castro; Marissa Castro; Frank Castrina; Judy Castrina; Diana Cohen; Jack Crump; Ken Daga; Jenny D'Arienzo; Sam Davis; Peter Delaney; Sarah Deprin; Chip Drysdale; Dianne Drysdale; Rhea Drysdale; to the memories of Shirley Duglin and Walter Duglin; Chadd Eaglin; Peter Eisenberg; Bill Falik; Susan Feingold; Emily Figdor; Isabella Figdor; Jeff Fleisser;

Judy Fox-Fleisser; Jamie Fletcher; to the memory of Rosemary Fletcher; Campbell Ford; to the memory of Gabe Friedberg; Helene Friedberg; James Friedberg; Rebecca Friedberg; Frank Friel; Norma Burak Friel; Jeff Garland: Stephanie Garland; to the memory of Doran George; Marla Golden; Hugh Greene; Jennifer Groccia; Deb Halpin; Deb Hardman; Cory Harris; Randy Harris; Roy Hinman; Joseph Hirsch; Kevin Hogencamp; to the memory of Jay Horowitz; Roberta Huberman; Ann Hunt; William Hunt; Carol Kafin; Robert Kafin; Lynn Keiner; Matt and Christina Keiner; Nick and Cristin Keiner; to the memory of Philip Keiner; Robert Keiner; John Kitzhaber; Susan Koehnel; Brian Kurz; Dennis Lang; Kathy Lang; Mirelle Lay; Steve Lay; Aiko Lee; John Lee; Anne Levkoff; Steve Levkoff; Issac Levy; Barbara Liwen; to the memory of Rachel Lufrano; Dorothy Martiesian; Terry Martiesian; Kirk McCombs; Greg McDaniel; Judy McDaniel; Mark McGowen; Mercedes McGowen; Mark Mcintosh; Scott Mendelson; Lanie Mensh; Ron Mensh; Emmy Michalakis; Jeff Nyman; Marilyn Nyman; to the memory of Helen Pezzulich; Bob Pezzulich; to the memory of Michael

Pruitt; Jack Porvaznik; Michele Remington; Steve Risen; Michelle Rosenbaum; Mike Rosenberg; Elias Rosenblatt; to the memory of Ruth Rosenblatt; to the memory of Bruce Samuels; Christine Sanders; Betsy Schifanella; Brenda Schonberg; Stu Schwartz; David Schwerin; Marlene Setzer; Atul Shah; Kathy Shapiro; Ron Shapiro; Bill Shivers; Eric Siegle; Jeff Siegle; Norah Siegle; Rabab Siegle; Wendy Smolens-Risen; Sue Snyder; Tom Snyder; Alyssa Spallone; Brenda Spallone; Joseph Spallone; Judy Steen; Kent Steen; John Tanner; Elizabeth Taylor; Bruce Tempest; Phyllis Tempest; Mark Tomaski; Bonnie Toole; Bahati Van Pelt; David Vilner; to the memory of Jan Weimer; Riko Weimer; Sandy Weimer; Edie Welty; Tom Welty; Dirk Wentdorf; Ken West; Shea Westfall; to the memory of Richard Winslow; Wissa Winslow; Steve Wise; Carolyn Woods; and Jeff Woods.

I do want to specially acknowledge a number of friends, all of whom gifted me with their talent, time, and kindness.

Amy Brenneman attributed my first book *The Cradle Will Fall* with helping her through postpartum depression. Over time we developed a long-distance phone friendship. I want to congratulate her on the publication of her excellent book about her experience entitled *Boxing the Blues Away,* with a forward by her "therapist," world champion boxer Roy Jones Jr. She was also kind enough to mention The Patients Party on her back cover.

Special thanks to David Deprin for his guidance through the maze of hospital finance (see Chapter 14).

Alan Halperin (contributor to this book -- see Chapter 5) and I have spent hundreds of miles walking and hundreds of hours talking about healthcare and life. A deep thinker and wise person, he has expanded my soul. I am very grateful.

Patrick Kelso is a talented technology wizard. Over many years he has helped Ronnie and I with our personal limitations in terms of dealing with technology in our home environment. Through the development of The Patients Party, his ideas and abilities have been increasingly valuable.

Special thanks to Robert Lufrano whose wisdom and expertise related to our healthcare system have been particularly valuable (see Chapter 3).

Robert (Robbie) Malvicino made the unlikely transition from playing professional soccer in Argentina, to international graphic/web designer based in St. Augustine, Florida. In 2011 Michelle Branham, a terrific marketing/ public relations professional (now working as VP of Policy for the Alzheimers Association)said simply, "don't hire anyone other than Robbie, he is fantastic." She was correct.

Jack McNeil has designed my last five books. However, his contributions go well beyond his graphic/artistic skills; he is an elegant and sensitive advisor, providing thoughtful insights that have added significantly to the quality of my work. Specifically, it is Jack's illustration that adorns the cover of *Patients Before Profits.* I am joyful that Jack is currently following his heart's path to be ordained in the Anglican Church.

In addition, I extend my respect to the memory of his wonderful father, Jack Sr., also my supporter and friend.

One day in the fall of 2014 Tom Schifanella and I were walking on the beach before work. We began to talk about a previous book *Medicine's Moral Mess.* As creative director of a very successful advertising firm in Jacksonville, he volunteered to provide the basic design for the cover (used in two previous books) in return for dinner (organic and farm to table). Recently, Tom decided to get serious about his long love of photography. He's actually pretty good. You can find some of his recent work in National Geographic.

Finally, in addition to those already mentioned, I acknowledge a very special team of people who have been very supportive and so generous with their time: Sally Dodge and Dale Guldbrandsen, (co-founders of The Patients Party); Mary Ann Aycock; Tom Aycock; Bob Blackman; Celeste Blackman; Alexandra Blackwell; Sharon Cobb; Jackie Corsey; Michael Colina; Dennis D'Arienzo; Ken Fink; Dick Fisher; Kathleen Halperin; Robin Halpin; Elizabeth Kaye; Patrick Kelso; Melissa Kurz; Emily Mesiano; Joe Schwarz; Judy Smith; Debra Tomaski; Randy Wainright, and finally, with deep love and appreciation, I honor the memory of Serena Lyde.

Bibliography

The bibliography below lists books and articles in chronological order that were mentioned in *Patients Before Profits,* as well as books not mentioned but consulted during the writing of this book.

1962 *Capitalism and Freedom* by Milton Freidman; University of Chicago Press; ISBN 978-0-226-26400-41970

1970 *Future Shock* by Alvin Toffler; Random House; ISBN 978-0-553-27737-1

1982 *The Social Transformation of American Medicine* by Paul Starr; Basic Books; ISBN 0–465–07935-0

1987 *Setting Limits: Medical Goals in an Aging Society* by Daniel Callahan; Simon and Schuster, Inc.; ISBN 0-671-22477-8

1992 *The Logic of Healthcare Reform* by Paul Starr; Whittle Books/Penguin; ISBN 0–14–023893-0

September 26, 1992 - Speech by Governor John Kitzhaber (M.D.) about the OREGON PLAN and rationing. Reprinted with permission.

1993 *Medicine at the Crossroads: The Crisis in Healthcare* by Melvin Konner, M.D.; Pantheon Books/Random House; ISBN 0– 679–41545–9

1994 *The Cradle Will Fall* by Carl S. Burak, M.D., J.D. and Michele G. Remington, Donald I. Fine, Inc. (Penguin), ISBN 1-55611-408-7

1996 *Please Don't Get Sick* by Albert Barnett Ferguson Jr., MD., FRCS (LOND.), HON., FACS;
Vantage Press; ISBN 0–533–11745 –3

1996 *Health Against Wealth: HMOs and The Breakdown of Medical Trust* by George Anders; Houghton Mifflin; ISBN 0–395– 82283-1

1997 *Market Driven Health Care* by Regina Herzlinger; Perseus Books, ISBN 0 –7382–0136-7

1998 *Conscious Capitalism: Principles for Prosperity* by David A. Schwerin; Butterworth-Heinemann; ISBN 0-7506-7021-5

1998 *Love and Survival: The Scientific Basis for the Healing Power of Intimacy* by Dean Ornish, M.D.; Harper Collins; ISBN 0-06-017213-4

1998, 2001, 2014 *The Power of Nice* by Ronald M. Shapiro and Mark A. Jankowski with James Dale; Wiley; ISBN 0-471-08072-1

1999 *The Dartmouth Atlas Of Healthcare* by John Wennberg, M.D. M.P.H., et al.; AHA Press, ISBN 1-55648-257-4

2001 *Crossing the Quality Chasm*: A New Health System for the 21st Century by the Institute of Medicine;National Academy Press; ISBN 0–309–07280–8

2001 *Professionalism: The Third Logic* by Eliot Freidson; The University of Chicago Press; ISBN 0–226–26203-0

2001 *The New Medicine: Life and Death After Hippocrates* by Nigel M. de S. Cameron; The Bioethics Press, LLC; ISBN 0-9711599-0-4

2003 *The Brave New World of Health Care* by Richard D. Lamm; Fulcrum Publishing; ISBN 1–5591–510–8

2003 *Health & Health Care*, Second Edition, by The Institute for the Future; Jossey Bass; ISBN 0–7879–5974-0

2003 "The Asheville Project: Long-Term Clinical and Economic Outcomes of a Community Pharmacy Diabetes Care Program" by Carol W. Cranor, PhD; Barry A. Bunting, PharmD; Dale B. Christensen, PhD; et al. Journal of the American Pharmacists Association, March-April 2003.

2003 *Health Care Meltdown; Confronting the Myths and Fixing Our Failing System* by Robert H. LeBow, M.D.; Alan C. Hood and Company; ISBN 0–911469–22–2

2003 "The Effect of Incentive-Based Formularies on Prescription-Drug Utilization and Spending" by Halden A. Hyskamp, Patricia A. Deverka, Arnold M. Epstein, et al. New England Journal of Medicine, December 4, 2003.

2004 *Critical Condition: How Health Care in America Became Big Business and Bad Medicine* by Donald L. Bartlett and James B. Steele; Doubleday/Random House; ISBN 0–385–50454-3

2004 *The Truth About Drug Companies: How They Deceive Us and What to Do About It* by Marcia Angell, M.D.; Random House; ISBN 0–375–50846–5

2004 "Bad Tiered Formulary Designs Yield Poor Outcomes, High Cost" by Martin Sipkoff, Managed Care Magazine, August 2004.

2004 *NHS plc: The Privatisation of Our Health Care (A British Perspective)* by Allyson M. Pollock; Verso; ISBN 1–84476–011-2

2004 *Overdosed America: The Broken Promise Of American Medicine* by John Abramson, M.D.; Harper Collins Publishers; ISBN 0-06–056852–6

2004 *The $800 Million Pill: The Truth Behind the Cost of New Drugs* by Merrill Goozner; University of California Press; ISBN 0–520–23945-8

2005 *On the Take: How Medicine's Complicity with Big Business Can Endanger Your Health* by Jerome P. Kassirer, M.D.; Oxford University Press; ISBN 0–19–517684–7

2005 *The Business of Healthcare Innovation* edited by Lawton Robert Burns; Cambridge University Press; ISBN 978–0–521–54768–0

2005 *One Nation Uninsured: Why the U.S. Has No National Health Insurance* by Jill Quadagno: Oxford University Press; ISBN 978-0-19-531203-4

2005 *Conscious Globalism: What's Wrong with the World and How to Fix It* by David A. Schwerin: Digital Junction Press; ISBN 978-09765189–3-8

2006 *Redefining Healthcare: Creating Value-Based Competition* by Michael E. Porter and Elizabeth Olmstead Teisberg; Harvard Business School Press; ISBN 978–1–59139–778-6

2006 *Money Driven Medicine: The Real Reason Healthcare Costs So Much* by Maggie Mahar; Collins; ISBN 978–0–06-076533

2006 *The Political Economy of Health Care: A Clinical Perspective* by Julian Tudor Hart; The Policy Press; ISBN 1– 86134 –809–6

2006 "Medicare Part D – The Product of a Broken Process" by Louise M. Slaughter, M.P.H.; New England Journal of Medicine, June 1, 2006.

2006 *When I Became a Psychiatrist, People Stopped Waving on Main Street* by Carl S. Burak, M.D., J.D.; Stanton and Samuel Publishing, ISBN 0-9723357-1-4

2007 *Who Killed Healthcare; America's $2 Trillion Medical Problem – and the Consumer-Driven Cure* by Regina Herzlinger; McGraw-Hill; ISBN 978–0–07–148780-1

2007 *Without Your Consent: The Hijacking of American Health Care* by Michael J. Newton, M.D.; Paribus Publishing; ISBN 1– 933705–11–6

2007 *Sick: The Untold Story of America's Health Care Crisis – and the People Who Pay the Price* by Jonathan Cohn; Harper Collins Publishers; ISBN 978–0–06–058045–2

2007 *Overtreated: Why Too Much Medicine Is Making Us Sicker and Poorer* by Shannon Brownlee; Bloomsbury USA; ISBN 1-58234-579-1

2007 *A Second Opinion: Rescuing America's Health Care* by Arnold S. Relman, M.D.; Public Affairs; ISBN 1-58648-481-8

2008 *Predictably Irrational: The Hidden Forces That Shape Our Decisions* by Dan Ariely; Harper/Harper Collins Publishers; ISBN 978–0–06–135323

2008 *Critical: What We Can Do About the Health-Care Crisis* by Tom Daschle, Scott S. Greenberger and Jeanne M. Lambrew; Thomas Dunne Books; ISBN 978-0-312-38302-5

2008 *Healthcare, Guaranteed: A Simple, Secure Solution for America* by Ezekiel J. Emanuel, M.D., Ph.D.; Public Affairs; ISBN 978-1-58648-662-4

2008 *The Philosophy of Medicine Reborn* by Edmund D. Pelligrino – Edited by H. Tristram Engelhardt and Fabrice Jotterand: University of Notre Dame Press; ISBN 13:978-0-268-03834-2

2008 *Hippocrates Shadow* by David H. Newman, M.D.; Scribner; ISBN 978-1-4165-5153-9

2008 *Nudge: Improving Decisions About Health, Wealth, and Happiness* by Richard H. Thaler and Cass R. Sunstein; ISBN 978-0-14-311526-7

2008 "The Great Seduction" by David Brooks; New York Times, June 10, 2008.

2008 *The Corrosion of Medicine: Can the Profession Reclaim Its Moral Legacy?*; by John Geyman, M.D.; Common Courage Press; ISBN 978-1-56751-384-4

2009 *Health Care Reform: The Truth* by Julio Gonzalez, M.D.; Aragon Publishers; ISBN 978-0-615-26746-3

2009 *Rx Too Much Medicine: A Doctor's Prescription for Better and More Affordable Health Care* by Dennis Gottfried M.D.; Paragon House; ISBN 978-1-55778-881-8

2009 *The Information Cure: Solving The Healthcare Crisis Systematically Through Integrated Healthcare Management* by Jeff Margolis; The TriZetto Group; ISBN 978-1-60743-391-0

2009 *Best Care Anywhere: Why VA Health Care Is Better Than Yours* by Phillip Longman; Berrett-Koehler Publishers; ISBN 978-0-9824171-5-7

2009 *The Healing of America: A Global Quest for Better, Cheaper, and Fairer Health Care* by T.R. Reid;
ISBN 978-1-59420-234-6

2009 *The Heart of Power: Health and Politics in the Oval Office* by David Blumenthal and James A. Morone; University of California Press; ISBN 978-0-520-26030-6

2009 "How Did Economists Get It So Wrong?" By Paul Krugman; New York Times Magazine, September 2, 2009.
2009 "Hope Springs Eternal" by Anna Quindlan; Newsweek, November 2, 2009.

2009 *Howard Dean's Prescription for Real Healthcare Reform: How We Can Achieve Affordable Medical Care for Every American and Make Our Jobs Safer* by Howard Dean, M.D. with Igor Volskyand Faiz Shakir; Chelsea Green Publishing Company; ISBN 978-1-60358-228-5

2009 *Getting What We Deserve: Health and Medical Care In America* by Alfred Sommer, M.D., M.H.S.; The Johns Hopkins University Press; ISBN 978-0-8018-9387-2

2009 *American Radical: The Life and Times of I.F. Stone* by D.D. Guttenplan; Farrar Strauss and Giroux;
ISBN 13: 978-0-374-18393-6

2009 *The Age of American Unreason* by Susan Jacoby; Vintage/ Random House; ISBN 978-1-4000-9638-1

2009 *The Innovator's Prescription: A Disruptive Solution for Healthcare* by Clayton M. Christensen, Jerome H. Grossman, M.D. & Jason Hwang, M.D.; McGraw Hill; ISBN 978-0-07-159208-6

2009 "The Cost Conundrum: What a Texas Town Can Teach Us About Healthcare" by Atul Gawande; New Yorker Magazine, June 1, 2009

2010 *Tracking Medicine: A Researcher's Quest to Understand Healthcare* by John E. Wennberg; Oxford University Press; ISBN 978-0-19-973178-7

2010 *White Coat Black Hat: Adventures on the Dark Side of Medicine* by Carl Elliott; Beacon Press; ISBN 978-0-8070-6144-2

2010 *Assholistic Healthcare: Healthcare Reform: Medicine's Moral Mess* by Carl S. Burak, M.D., J.D.; Stanton and Samuel Publishing; ISBN 978-0-9723357-4-4

2010 *Health Care Reform and American Politics: What Everyone Needs to Know* by Lawrence R. Jacobs and Theda Skocpol; Oxford University Press; ISBN 978-0-19-976912-4

2010 *Fresh Medicine: How to Fix Reform and Build a Sustainable Health Care System* by Philip Bredesen; Atlantic Monthly Press; ISBN 978-0-8021-1938-4

2010 *Getting It Done: How Obama and Congress Finally Broke the Stalemate to Make Way for Health Care Reform* by Tom Daschle with David Nather; Thomas Dunne Books, St. Martins Press; ISBN 978-0-312-64378-2

2010 *The New Healthcare System: Everything You Need to Know* by David Nather; Thomas Dunne Books / St. Martin's Press; ISBN 978-0-312-64934-0

2010 *Demand Better: Revive Our Broken Healthcare System* by Sanjaya Kumar, M.D., M.Sc., M.P.H. and David Nash M.D., M.B.A; Second River Healthcare Press: ISBN 13: 978-1-936406-01-2

2010 *Freefall: America, Free Markets, and The Sinking of the World Economy* by Joseph E. Stiglitz; W.W. Norton and Company: ISBN 978-0-393-07596-0

2010 *Sick & Tired: How America's Health Care System Fails Its Patients* by Helene Jorgensen; PoliPoint Press LLC: ISBN 978-0-9824171-1-9

2011 *Health Care Reform; What It Is – Why It's Necessary – How It Works* by Jonathan Gruber with H.P. Newquist; Illustrated by Nathan Schreiber; Hill and Wang – A Division of Farrar, Straus and Giroux: ISBN 978-0-8090-5397-1

2011 *Breaking Point: How the Primary Care Crisis Endangers the Lives of Americans* by John Geyman, M.D.; Copernicus Healthcare; ISBN 978-0-9837734-0-5

2011 *Power, Politics, and Universal Health Care: The Inside Story of a Century-Long Battle* by Stuart Altman and David Schactman; Prometheus Books; ISBN 978-1-61614-456-2

2011 *How We Do Harm: A Doctor Breaks Ranks About Being Sick In America* by Otis Webb Brawley, M.D. with Paul Goldberg;St. Martins Press; ISBN 978-0-312-67297-3

2011 *The Hippocratic Myth: Why Doctors Are Under Pressure To Ration Care, Practice Politics, And Compromise Their Promise To Heal* by M. Gregg Bloch, M.D.: Palgrave Macmillan; ISBN 978-0-230-60373-8

2011 *Thinking Fast and Slow* by Daniel Kahneman; Farrar, Straus and Giroux; ISBN 978-0-374-27563-1

2011 *The Better Angels of Our Nature: Why Violence Has Declined* by Steven Pinker; Penguin; ISBN 978-0-14-312201-2

2012 *Unaccountable: What Hospitals Won't Tell You and How Transparency Can Revolutionize Health Care* by Marty Makary, M.D.; Bloomsbury Press; ISBN 978-1-60819-836-8

2012 *What Money Can't Buy: The Moral Limits of Markets* by Michael J. Sandel; Farrar, Strauss and Giroux; ISBN 978-0-374-20302-0

2012 *The Measure of a Nation* by Howard Steven Friedman; Prometheus Books; ISBN 928-1-61614-569-9

2012 *The Blood Sugar Solution* by Mark Hyman, M.D.; Little Brown; ISBN 978-0-316-12737-0

2012 *The Creative Destruction of Medicine* by Eric Topol, M.D.; Basic Books; ISBN 978-0-465-02550-3

2012 "Medicare Bills Rise as Records Turn Electronic" by Reed Abelson, Julie Creswell and Griffin J. Palmer; New York Times, September 22, 2012.

2012 *Abundance: The Future Is Better Than You Think* by Peter H. Diamandis and Steven Kotler; Free Press; ISBN 978-1-4516-1421-3

2012 *The Blue Zones* Second Edition by Dan Buettner; National Geographic: ISBN 978-1-4262-0948-2

2013 "Failure to Launch? The Independent Payment Advisory Board's Uncertain Prospects" by Jonathan Oberlander, Ph.D. and Marisa Morrison, B.A.; New England Journal of Medicine, July 11, 2013.

2013 *The American Health Care Paradox: Why Spending More Is Getting Us Less* by Elizabeth H. Bradley and Lauren A. Taylor; Public Affairs; ISBN 978-1-61039-209-9

2013 "Bitter Pill: Why Medical Bills Are Killing Us" by Steven Brill; Time Magazine, March 4, 2013

2013 *David and Goliath: Underdogs, Misfits, and the Art of Battling Giants* by Malcolm Gladwell; Little Brown: ISBN 978-0-316-20436-1

2014 *Medical Madness: Meet the Golden Rule* by George Huber; Author House: ISBN 978-1-4969-1980-9

2014 *Doctored: The Disillusionment of an American Physician* by Sandeep Jauhar; Farrar, Straus and Giroux: ISBN 978-0-374-14139-4

2015 *The Patient Will See You Now: The Future of Medicine Is in Your Hands* by Eric Topol; Basic Books: ISBN 978-0-465-05474-9

2015 *America's Bitter Pill: Money, Politics, Backroom Deals, and the Fight to Fix Our Broken Healthcare System* by Steven Brill; Random House: ISBN 978-0-8129-9695-1

2015 *Bold: How to Go Big, Create Wealth and Impact the World* by Peter H. Diamandis and Steven Kotler; Simon & Schuster: ISBN 978-1-4767-0956-7

2015 *Misbehaving: The Making of Behavioral Economics* by Richard H. Thaler; W. W. Norton and Company; ISBN 978-0-393-35279-5

2015 "Overkill: An Avalanche of Medical Care Is Harming Patients Physically and Financially. What Can We Do About It?" By Atul Gawande; New Yorker Magazine, May 11, 2015.

2015 *Health, Medicine and Justice: Designing a Fair and Equitable Healthcare System* by Joshua Freeman, M.D.; Copernicus Healthcare: ISBN 978-0-9887996-8-4

2015 *Saving Capitalism: For the Many Not the Few* by Robert B. Reich; Penguin Random House; ISBN 978-0-3853-5057-0

2015 *Sapiens: A Brief History of Humankind* by Yuval Noah Harari; Harper Perennial; ISBN 978-0-06-231611-0

2016 *Medicine's Moral Mess: Why the Delivery of Healthcare in the United States Must Change* by Carl S. Burak; Stanton and Samuel Publishing; ISBN 978-0-9723357-0-6

2016 *Thank You for Being Late: An Optimist's Guide to Thriving in the Age of Accelerations* by Thomas L. Friedman; Farrar, Straus and Giroux; ISBN 978-0-374-27353-8

2017 *Mistreated: Why We Think We're Getting Good Health Care – and Why We're Usually Wrong* by Robert Pearl, MD; Public Affairs; ISBN-13: 978-1-61039-765-0

2017 *An American Sickness: How Healthcare Became Big Business and How You Can Take It Back* by Elisabeth Rosenthal; Penguin Press; ISBN 978-1-59420-675-7

2017 *Economics for the Common Good* by Jean Tirole; Princeton University Press; IBN 978-0-691-17516-4

2017 *The Blue Zones of Happiness: Lessons from the World's Happiest People* by Dan Buettner; National Geographic; ISBN 978-1-4262-1848-4

2017 *Better Now: Six Big Ideas to Improve Health Care for All Canadians* by Dr. Danielle Martin; Allen Lane/Penguin Random House; ISBN 978-0-7352-3259-4

2018 *AI Superpowers: China, Silicon Valley and the New World Order* by Kai-Fu Lee; Houghton Mifflin Harcourt; ISBN 978-1-328-54639-5

2018 *Can Democracy Survive Global Capitalism?* by Robert Kuttner; W.W. Norton and Company; ISBN 978-0-393-60993-6

2018 *Winners Take All: The Elite Charade of Changing the World* by Anand Giridharadas; Alfred A. Knopf; ISBN 978-0-451-49324-8

2018 *How to Change Your Mind: What the New Science of Psychedelics Teaches Us About Consciousness, Dying, Addiction, Depression, and Transcendence* by Michael Pollan; Penguin Press; ISBN 978-1-59420-422-7

2018 *Overcharged : Why Americans Pay Too Much for Health Care* by Charles Silver and David A. Hyman; Cato Institute; ISBN 978-1944424-76-3

2019 "The Impossible Medicare For All " by David Brooks; *The New York Times;* March 5, 2019

2019 *The Second Mountain: The Quest for a Moral Life* by David Brooks; Random House; ISBN 978-0-8129-9326-4

2019 *Know Your Soul: Bring Joy to Your Life* by Diana Muenz Chen and David A. Schwerin, with a message from Archangel Michael; Allone Press; ISBN 978-0-9765189-1-4

2019 *Priced Out: The Economic and Ethical Costs of American Health Care* by Uwe E. Reinhardt; Princeton University Press; ISBN 978-0-691-19217-8

2019 *Deep Medicine/How Artificial Intelligence Can Make Healthcare Human Again* by Eric Topol; Basic Books; ISBN 978-1-5416-4463-2

Made in United States
North Haven, CT
04 November 2026

21770482R00199

2019 *The Rabbit Effect: Live Longer, Happier, and Healthier with the Groundbreaking Science of Kindness* by Kelli Harding, MD, MPH; Atria Books; ISBN 978-1-5011-8426-0

2019 *People, Power, and Profits: Progressive Capitalism for An Age of Discontent* by Joseph Stiglitz; W.W. Norton & Company; ISBN 978-0-393-35833-9

2019 Compassionomics: The Revolutionary Scientific Evidence That Caring Makes A Difference by Stephen Trzeciak and Anthony Mazzarelli; Studer Group; ISBN 978-1-62218-106-3

2020 *Economic Dignity* by Gene Sperling; Penguin Press; ISBN 978-1-9848-7987-5

2020 "No Vaccine in Sight: The U.S. was Once at the Cutting Edge of Pandemic Protection. Then Big Pharma Took Over." By Alexander Zaitchik; The New Republic; June 2020

2020 *The Long Fix: Solving America's Health Care Crisis with Strategies That Work for Everyone* by Vivian S. Lee, MD; W.W. Norton & Company; ISBN 978-1-324-00667-1

2020 *Which Country Has the World's Best Healthcare?* by Ezekiel J. Emanuel ; Public Affairs; ISBN-13: 978-1-5417-9773-4

2020 *First Principles; What America's Founders Learned from the Greeks and Romans and How That Shaped our Country* by Thomas E. Ricks; Harper Collins; ISBN 978-0-06-299745-6

PATIENTS BEFORE PROFITS

Make America Compassionate Again

CARL S. BURAK

Stanton & Samuel

Production management: Stanton and Samuel Publishing LLC
Cover & Book Design: Jack McNeil, Jacksonville, FL
Authors Photo: Ronnie Burak, Atlantic Beach, Florida

First edition: May, 2021
Library of Congress Catalog-in-Publication Data: Request from publisher

Burak, Carl S., 1942-

Patients Before Profits; Make America Compassionate Again: healthcare reform, health; preventive medicine; integrative medicine; kindness; compassionate; happiness. 1st ed. Additional data available upon request.

Includes bibliographic references. ISBN 978-0-9723357-5-1 (soft cover)

1. Compassion and society. 2. Acceleration of Society. 3. Medical care—United States. 4. Health care reform—United States. 5. Insurance, Health—United States. 1. Title

DNLM: 1. Compassion and Society—profound societal acceleration. 2. Happiness—World. 3. Insurance, Health—United States. 4. Delivery of Health Care—economics—United States. 5. Free Market Disfunction—United States 6. Health Care Reform—United States. 7. Universal Coverage—United States.

10 9 8 7 6 5 4 3 2 1

Also by Carl S. Burak

The Cradle Will Fall (with Michele Remington)

When I Became a Psychiatrist People Stopped Waving on Main Street

Assholistic Healthcare

Medicine's Moral Mess

The Answer to Medicine's Moral Mess: Medicare for All

Dr. Medicare: Make America Compassionate Again

Table of Contents

Dedication

To my grandchildren, Ani Blaze Burakian and Levon Sage Burakian, whose very existence and joyous spirits bring me peace and happiness. And to my patients, who taught me so much. All patients deserve better from America, a nation so blessed.

The best things in life aren't things.

–Ann Landers

Introduction

I am in the autumn of my years. What does that mean? It means I'm older but still a little colorful. It also means that I was born in Philadelphia, Pennsylvania, on November 20, 1942, the exact same day that President Biden was born in Scranton. Maybe there was something about that day.

The president and I have had different journeys. From early on, he had gifts of leadership and persuasion that were far above my pay grade. I believe he has an extraordinary capacity for resilience that allowed him to continue his journey despite the loss of his wife, his daughter, and later his son Beau. But I believe we

have both traveled a path that was filled with desire to serve humanity in a way that is larger than our individual lives.

There are probably other observations I could make that I won't, except to honor our wives and relationships. Jill Biden, who Joe met and married some years after he lost his wife and daughter, has been described by the president as "the person who allowed me to dream again." Dr. Jill Biden has worked as a respected educator, and when I see them together, I see a couple who are true partners.

When Ronnie and I married almost fifty-three years ago, I had just received my MD and she her Bachelor of Fine Arts. That she was destined to earn a PhD (like Jill) and become Dr. Burak, a respected psychologist, was not predictable at the time. It is my hope, however, that aside from the doctoral educations of Jill and Ronnie, people looking at Ronnie and I would also see a couple who are true partners.

In these autumn years, I am too old to beat around the bush. My life journey ultimately provided a background that supported my desire to expand my playing field, to understand American uniqueness

especially from our current canyon of partisanship, and most of all to appreciate what it means to "be well."

Over the years, the opportunity to help patients has nourished my soul, and I am grateful. I would have been happy practicing until I ran out of steam, but about a dozen years ago I woke up to the realization that American healthcare had significant problems. I began exploring.

The deeper I dove, the more passionate I became. Finally realizing that I could not fully pursue this path while continuing to practice, I retired at age seventy-five, with both regret and excitement.

Over these dozen years, I wrote a succession of books: *Assholistic Healthcare; Medicine's Moral Mess; The Answer to Medicine's Moral Mess,* and *Dr Medicare.* Over time I estimate about a couple thousand readings occurred, and I received valuable feedback.

These books were, in retrospect, milestones of my self-directed personal graduate education. Speaking only for myself, although I had been a doctor for forty years when I began to walk this path, I had surprisingly little wisdom or understanding of the system I was working in and for.

One thing this journey has suggested is that despite the legislative complexity of our healthcare, symbolized by the two thousand plus pages of the Affordable Care Act, core principles necessary to devise a truly excellent, compassionate, and less expensive system need not be that complicated. It is the sausage grinder of politics that makes progress difficult. America has enormous potential to improve healthcare and refresh the American dream – dual issues that may be more related than we think.

Chapter 16 includes this brief vignette:

> According to a Jeffrey Toobin *The New Yorker* article (Dec. 24 & 31, 2018), an unlikely dinner grouping occurred a few years back that included Senator John McCain, Congressman Adam Schiff, the singer Bono, and Bill Gates. Following one of many shared jokes, possibly one about being of Irish descent, Bono said, "You know I love Ireland, I'm a proud Irishman. Ireland is a great country, but it's not an idea. America is not just a country; it's an idea."

I have been thinking about America as an idea, a conceptual space, trying to understand how our humanity and laws and economy and values relate, especially to our current partisanship. The recent insurrection and breach of the Capitol was heartbreaking.

America the idea was an exceptional (but perhaps partly accidental) gift from our Founding Fathers. Built upon the wisdom memorialized by the Declaration of Independence and the Constitution, these men dreamed principles of governance that embraced equality, creative diversity, and human uniqueness; but their initial attempt to manifest these aspirational principles were at best farcical, and at worst deplorable.

Although the founders espoused equality between all "men," their working model at the time fell egregiously short; women, Original Americans, and slaves were not included.

We also developed a far less then perfect system of law (as all legal systems inherently are), but one that is at least philosophically flexible and has the potential to be enlightened and encourage a degree of fairness and civility.

Finally, we've created mildly idiosyncratic and misunderstood principles of commerce and economy.

My thoughts about health, humanity, the law, and economic reality have been informed by an educational and personal journey that I wouldn't have been able to predict as a medical student. The path I've followed was not expected.

If you choose to take this journey with me, you are likely to find ideas that you disagree with. I will tell you right now that my ideas do not reflect unassailable truth. My ideas are not sacrosanct. Despite my various educational and life experiences I am profoundly ignorant. So are you. The amount we know in this life, this world, this universe is tiny compared to what we don't know.

Our ignorance is nourished in part by the limitations of our perception: Dogs hear sounds that we don't; there are colors all around us that we can't see; and there's jazz music playing in my study and your space, music that you and I can't hear because we haven't turned on the radio. We can't hear it, but it exists – it is real.

The deficiencies of our perceptions cause us to

be limited in our conceptual thinking. We're missing important information. There are probably dimensions of time and space and who knows what else that we can't appreciate. Emotional states also contort ideas. But we have magic.

Despite our limited boundaries, our minds have some capacity to expand, to imagine sometimes accurately what lies outside our apparent limitations and conceive what is difficult to confirm.

The idea of America is still a work in progress. It took a few hundred years to begin moving forward with equality, and we're still struggling. However, I believe we are inching our way towards a more compassionate and unique "melting pot."

Each of us is also a work in progress. Each life is different, connected to the universe of possibility and comprehension in different ways.

Age confers both burden and advantage. I think I'm a slow bloomer. As I've lived longer, I am better able to focus on being well. I think I am better able to be me.

One of my goals from the beginning was to tie the words of this book and the insights of my journey into